Damian Strohmeyer

A DAY IN THE LIFE OF THE
National Hockey League

CONTRIBUTING WRITERS

Frank Brown • Roy Cummings • Lisa Dillman • Pat Hickey • Len Hochberg

Tom McMillan • Nancy Marrapese • Scott Morrison

Brian Scrivener • Jim Taylor

HarperCollins*Publishers*Ltd

AN OPUS BOOK

Published in Canada by HarperCollins Publishers Ltd.

Created and produced by Opus Productions Inc.
300 West Hastings Street, Vancouver, British Columbia, Canada V6B 1K6

A DAY IN THE LIFE OF THE NHL © 1996 NHL Enterprises, Inc. and Opus Productions Inc.

First Edition

Canadian Cataloguing in Publication Data
Main entry under title: A day in the life of the NHL
ISBN 0-00-255723-1
1. National Hockey League. 2. National Hockey League - Pictorial works.

Table of Contents

NATIONAL HOCKEY LEAGUE ● NORTH AMERICA ● MARCH 23: 12:00 AM EST - 11:59 PM PST

Gary Bettman *Commissioner, NHL*

Foreword

Welcome. We at the National Hockey League are thrilled that

you are joining us for one of our typical great days of hockey – in this case, March 23, 1996.

Steve Solomon *Senior V.P. and COO, NHL*

• From British Columbia to Newfoundland and South Florida to Southern California, more people are playing hockey, more people are watching hockey, and more people are reading about hockey than ever before. *A Day in the Life of the NHL* reflects that enthusiasm for "the Coolest Game On earth." • In this book, 80 brilliant photographers and 10 outstanding hockey writers give you an all-access pass to the teams, players, fans, and families as they've never been seen.

Brian Burke *Senior V.P. and Director of Operations, NHL (left)*,
David Nonis *Manager, Hockey Operations, NHL*

You will warm up with the NHL players before their games, catch a glimpse of team strategy sessions, sit with the players on the bench, travel with the teams as they criss-cross North America, and share

Left to right: **Steve Solomon** *Senior V.P. and COO, NHL,* **Rick Dudley**
President, NHL Enterprises, **Richard Zahnd** *Senior V.P. and General
Counsel, NHLE,* **Doug Perlman** *Associate Counsel, NHLE,*
Charlie Schmitt *Director of Publishing, NHLE*

private moments with players and their families. • On the ice you will experience the intensity of the day's nine games – the heat of the Bruins-Rangers rivalry and the heart-stopping action as Pittsburgh's Mario Lemieux bears down on Buffalo's Dominik Hasek in one of hockey's most

thrilling moments, the penalty shot. Off the ice, you will see the events that surround the NHL – such as the first stop on the NHL BREAKOUT '96 tour – and spend a day with the Stanley Cup. • Working together, Opus

Elle Farrell *Manager, Publishing, NHLE*
Arthur Pincus *V.P. Public Relations, NHL*

Productions, HarperCollinsPublishers, the National Hockey League, and its players, have given the

Commissioner **Gary Bettman** *(left) and*
Jeffery Pash *Senior V.P. and General Counsel, NHL*

fans an extraordinary opportunity to take a transcontinental tour of the game we love so much. Throughout this portrait of the dreams and the dreamers, you will come to understand our devotion to the sport. • I would like to take this opportunity

to express sincere thanks to all the teams and players for their participation in this project and for making you, the fans, feel welcome inside their world. • Enjoy your trip.

Gary B. Bettman

Long before dawn on Saturday, March 23, 1996,

the first of 80 of the world's finest photographers began their work,

recording the earliest moments of *A Day in the Life of the National Hockey League*. By sunrise, the silent

army of NHL players and their families, management, officials, support staff, fans, and media, was in full

swing, preparing for games and practices that lay ahead. For all those involved in the creation of this book,

it was a revelation. For some of the action photographers, hockey is their beat; they enjoyed this

opportunity to put a slightly different focus on a familiar subject. For other photographers, new to the

game, the passion which hockey inspires – not just in NHLers but in minor hockey players of every age,

in fans, and everyone else it touches, from the largest city to the smallest town – was astonishing. For the

hockey writers, this Day was an opportunity to explore some of the larger themes about the game that

fall outside the day-to-day stories. Through the words and pictures that follow, we hope you will enjoy

Above

NIGHT SHIFT   3:55 am **EST**

Bleary-eyed and weary after flying through the night from Winnipeg, where the Philadelphia Flyers fell to the Winnipeg Jets 4-1 on Friday evening, the Flyers equipment crew has one more duty to perform before they can turn in. Arriving in their rental truck from Toronto's Pearson International Airport long before dawn, they must unload the team's equipment and stow it safely in the visitors' dressing room at Maple Leaf Gardens, where the Flyers and the Leafs will match up tonight. Left to right: Head trainer David Settlemyre, his son, Derek, and Jim Evers.

Paul Orenstein

Left

RELIGIOUS CONVERSION   12:01 am **EST**

As March 23 begins, crews in cities around North America are already hard at work converting NHL arenas to their hockey configuration from concerts, trade shows, or basketball games held Friday evening. At Pittsburgh Civic Arena, a Christian Ministries event ended before midnight. Before noon, the Pittsburgh Penguins must have the ice surface available for their morning skate. In little more than 18 hours, the Arena will host a game between the Penguins and the Buffalo Sabres. The Arena's operations manager, Sam Aceti, and his crew of 12 set to work. First they strike the conference stage; then they lift the four-by-eight-foot sheets of insulation covering the ice surface. Next, the rinkside glass and players' and penalty boxes are installed. The hockey set-up in place, they turn their attention to the ice surface, trimming it and flooding it to build it up to game standards. At the end of an eight-hour shift, their work is done.

Andy Levin

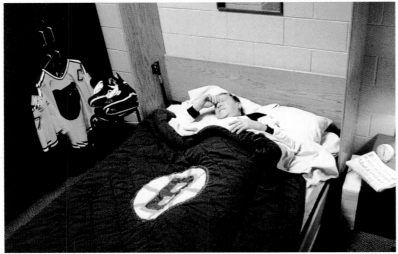

Steve Babineau

William DeKay

Judy Griesedieck

Andrew Stawicki

SUNRISE *Early morning*	**THE DAY BEGINS** *Early morning*

As day breaks throughout North America, hockey people are stirring. Top left: Boston Bruins equipment manager Ken Fleger wakes in his bedroom, located right in the training area of the FleetCenter arena where the Bruins play their home games. Bottom left: Members of the Saskatoon, Saskatchewan, Over 60 Oldtimers' hockey league – its name refers to the players' minimum age – board the bus taking them to the Annual Playmakers Tournament in Victoria, British Columbia. For the first year, the tournament will hold a competition for teams of players over 70 years old, like 79-year-old Fred Dawes (front row center), whose younger brother, Bobby, played for the Canadiens and Maple Leafs from 1946 to 1951.

The business of the NHL – official and not-so-official – gets an early start. Top right: Benny Ercolani, the NHL's official statistician, reviews statistics from Friday night's games on his home computer, assisted by his daughter Erica and her dog Homer. Bottom right: Hero worship: A young boy works up the courage to ask for an autograph from Toronto Maple Leafs star Wendel Clark (right), at breakfast with Don Meehan, player agent for Clark and many other NHL stars, such as Trevor Linden, Pat LaFontaine, and Jason Arnott.

The game of hockey is flourishing in Texas since the Stars came to Dallas in 1993.
Pictured is one of 50 youth hockey teams that take part in games held at the
Dr Pepper StarCenter in Valley Ranch, a suburb of Dallas, which the Stars use
as their practice facility. This winter, some 800 players between the ages of four
and 17 were registered in the StarCenter's league, with another 350 on the waiting
list. "Kids from up north whose families move to this area think they'll just step
in and clean up," says Dallas Stars hockey programs manager, Jouni Lehtola,
"but they're surprised at the high level of play they find here."

Facing page

WORLD'S BIGGEST STICK   9:40 am **CST**

Citizens of Eveleth, Minnesota, home of the U.S. Hockey Hall of Fame, pose proudly beside what they claim to be "the world's biggest hockey stick." Although another stick in North Cowichan, British Columbia, at 205 feet, is actually longer, it is made up of two parts put together, whereas this stick is all one piece. With a shaft 90 feet long and a blade of 17 feet, its proportions are identical to normal-sized sticks made by Christian Bros. of nearby Warroad, MN. To make the illusion complete, a five-foot-wide, 600-pound puck rests in front of the blade, and a mural depicting a goalie in his crease is painted on the facing wall of a nearby building.

Layne Kennedy

Above

ICE HOCKEY IN HARLEM   11:00 am **EST**

On the streets of New York City, the game of hockey is afoot. Here, one player heads home from an early morning game at the Lasker ice rink in Central Park. Ice Hockey in Harlem is a program which brings inner-city kids an opportunity to play the game, learning valuable lessons in teamwork and community service.

Andy Uzzle

Showdown in Beantown

It has been exactly eight weeks since Bruins captain Raymond Bourque and Rangers captain Mark Messier were Eastern Conference teammates in the All-Star Game at Boston's FleetCenter, where Messier set up Bourque on the winning goal. Now they are back on opposing sides. It's obvious Bourque and Messier share the same high moral standards, the same quest to be the best. "We're similar in a lot of ways," says Bourque. "We love the game and we still have the fire, and it's driven us to be successful all these years. But he's got six Cups and I don't." ● They have had distinguished parallel careers, but when people talk about the two of them, it's about their leadership. "Everyone knows he's there and reads off him," said Rangers defenseman Brian Leetch of Messier. "You come to the locker room and look at him and see how he's feeling and say, 'That's the way I feel today.' It's definitely a gift." Bruin right wing Rick Tocchet, who played with Messier on teams such as the Canada Cup and the Gretzky tour in 1994, calls Messier the best leader in pro sports. "He's got a calmness about him," said Tocchet. "When he walks in and puts on his skates, you feel as if you have a good chance to win because this guy is in the lineup." Boston goalie Bill Ranford, who played with Messier in Edmonton, says, "He just had that aura about him, that will to win. He had the ability to cause everyone else to raise up their game a level. Then, if you didn't, he let you know." ● Bourque has a similar impact on his teammates, but he is a different kind of a leader. He can be vocal in the dressing room, but he said it's a role he has had to grow into. "I lead by example, whether it is how I conduct myself around the room or off the ice. I want to make sure other guys don't look at me and think, 'He wasn't there tonight,' or 'He could've been better.' " ● It's been difficult for Bourque this season. He has been playing better than 30 minutes a game, and has had to play hard every shift, every night in order for his team to even have a chance to win. "When you're struggling all year, it's tough," he says. "Still, on the ice people look at me in practice and in games and say, 'Hey, that's what it takes, that's what you have to do to be successful.' " ● Bourque knows part of his role is to decide what's necessary to say and then say it. It's a matter of being part-psychologist, part-friend, and partly someone else's conscience, if that's what's needed. "It's tough for me to do," he says. "I'm worried about feelings too much ... about hurting somebody." While it seems to come more easily to Messier – with his famous stare that can bore holes through steel – he says it doesn't. "You try to help each other. If it's necessary [to be critical], you have to do it. That's sometimes the ugly part of the game. But if you're genuine in your approach and the bottom line is you care about winning, and that's the only thing that matters, then everything else will be clear."

Facing page

PROFILES IN COURAGE   *1st Period*

The two captains – Boston Bruins Ray Bourque (left) and New York Rangers Mark Messier – inspire their teammates with their stellar play on ice. But off the ice they show their true leadership. When it counts, they voice their opinions in the locker room, and others pay heed. Their point production ranks them both in the top 10 of all time. Messier's four points today give him 1,466, while Bourque scored his 1,300th and 1,301st.

Damian Strohmeyer

*On game day morning, New York Rangers
celebrated superfan, Larry Goodman,
jumps for joy against the backdrop of the
Manhattan skyline. Goodman usually
reserves his infectious enthusiasm for
Rangers home games at Madison
Square Garden, where he is well
known as "The Dancing Fan."*

Brian Smale

Long before game time, the FleetCenter is abuzz with activity.
Above left: *Bruins equipment manager Ken Fleger is in his 30th
year in hockey and his 17th in the NHL. Before coming to Boston
he was equipment manager for the Canucks and Devils, and for
Team Canada internationally.* Above right: *For a team meeting,
Boston Bruins assistant coach Cap Raeder pens a few points
about the Rangers style of play that his players need to keep in
mind for today's game.* Left: *Marty McSorley inspects his newly
sharpened skates to make sure the edge is keen. Ten days ago,
McSorley wore the colors of the Los Angeles Kings, which he had
done for most of the last eight seasons since arriving as part of the
trade that brought Wayne Gretzky to L.A. Now a Ranger, he is
reunited with Mark Messier, another of his old teammates from
the Stanley Cup-winning Oiler teams of the late eighties.*

Steve Babineau

FLYING FINN
1st Period

In just his third game as a Ranger since coming across from the Kings with Marty McSorley and Shane Churla on March 14, Jari Kurri (above) is still working to find his place within the Rangers system. A longtime linemate for Wayne Gretzky, in Edmonton and Los Angeles, Kurri, with 582 goals going into tonight's game, is third only behind Leafs Mike Gartner and The Great One among active career goal scorers. The Rangers have stocked their team with superstars this season in an attempt to recapture the Stanley Cup glory they so briefly experienced in 1994. All season long they have danced atop the standings, vying with Pittsburgh and Philadelphia for first place in the Eastern Conference. In today's game, they fly into the lead on a goal by Mark Messier just 35 seconds after the first face-off. Their potent first line adds two more before the Bruins can reply: a late first-period goal from Adam Graves and a mid-second-period power-play goal by Luc Robitaille, another former Gretzky linemate in Los Angeles.

Steve Babineau

ON THE MOVE
2nd Period

Bruins center Todd Elik eludes Mark Messier. Elik assisted on Heinze's second goal, and on Ray Bourque's second-period goal that gave the Bruins the lead. A much traveled, seven-year NHL veteran, Elik made stops at Los Angeles, Minnesota, Edmonton, San Jose, and St. Louis before coming to Boston this season. Playing with the likes of Heinze, Oates, and Bourque has rekindled Elik's scoring touch. After this day's game his points total 41, equal to his career high, with 10 games left to go.

Brian Babineau

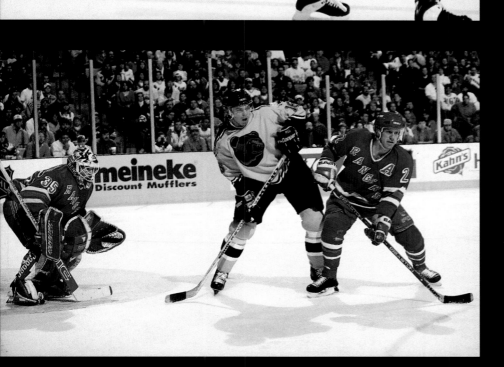

Top: *When his team needs leadership, Ray Bourque (left) responds. Here he moves in on defenseman Jeff Beukeboom in front of the Rangers' net. A gifted defenseman with offensive skills, having Bourque on your team is like having an extra forward on the ice.* Center: *Bruins centerman Jozef Stumpel sets up in front of Rangers goalie Mike Richter. Stumpel had five shots on goal in the game and assisted on Bourque's go-ahead goal at 8:15 of the third period. A native of Nitra, Slovakia, Stumpel was selected by the Bruins 40th overall in the 1991 Entry Draft, but this is his second full season with the club. He has responded to the opportunity, and is closing in on 50 points on the season. Here, he is closely watched by Rangers All-Star veteran defenseman Brian Leetch. The Rangers star played one season for Boston College before joining the U.S. National team in time for the 1988 Winter Olympics in Calgary. Leetch, who captained the Olympic squad, then went directly to the Rangers for the balance of the 1987-88 season. The next year he won the Calder Trophy as outstanding rookie, and since then has remained among the league's elite defensemen winning the Norris Trophy as the league's best in 1992. His superior ability came to the fore in the Rangers' 1994 run to the Stanley Cup, when Leetch scored 11 goals and 23 assists on his way to winning the Conn Smythe Trophy.*

Damian Strohmeyer

Watching his team fall behind 3-0 by 12:59 of the second period, Bruins head coach Steve Kasper (right) and his assistant Cap Raeder consider a change in strategy. In his nine-year career as a player with the Bruins, Kasper was one of the best defensive forwards in the league, winning the Frank J. Selke Trophy in 1981-82. Adjusting to the rigors of NHL coaching is a fresh challenge. His ascent to the top of professional hockey coaching ranks has been rapid. A player through 1992-93, he became Bruins assistant coach for the 1993-94 season, then moved on to lead the American Hockey League Providence Bruins, Boston's top farm team, in 1994-95. The parent club liked his winning style, and awarded him with his present position in May of 1995.

Steve Babineau

Above

IT'S A NATURAL

3rd Period

The outcome is often unpredictable in the NHL. An upset can happen in any game, and often from an unlikely source. Today, Steve Heinze, who previously had scored only 11 goals all season long, countered the Rangers with a natural hat trick, scoring two late-second-period goals and another (above), at 3:07 of the third, to tie the game 3-3. Perhaps it was the hometown crowd that inspired Heinze, who honed his hockey skills in the Boston area. A native of nearby Lawrence, Massachusetts, Heinze was a standout on the hockey team at perennial powerhouse Boston College before joining the Bruins after a brief stint on the U.S. Olympic team in 1992.

Brian Babineau

Left

FEARSOME DUO

2nd Period

Adam Graves (left) loads the gun and Mark Messier (right) pulls the trigger, Graves being the set-up man on many of his linemate's goals. Today, Messier returned the favor, assisting on Graves's goal at 14:52 of the first period. Also a member of the legendary 1990 Oilers team, Graves is a three-time winner of the Rangers' Steven McDonald "Extra Effort" Award for play "above and beyond the call of duty."

Steve Babineau

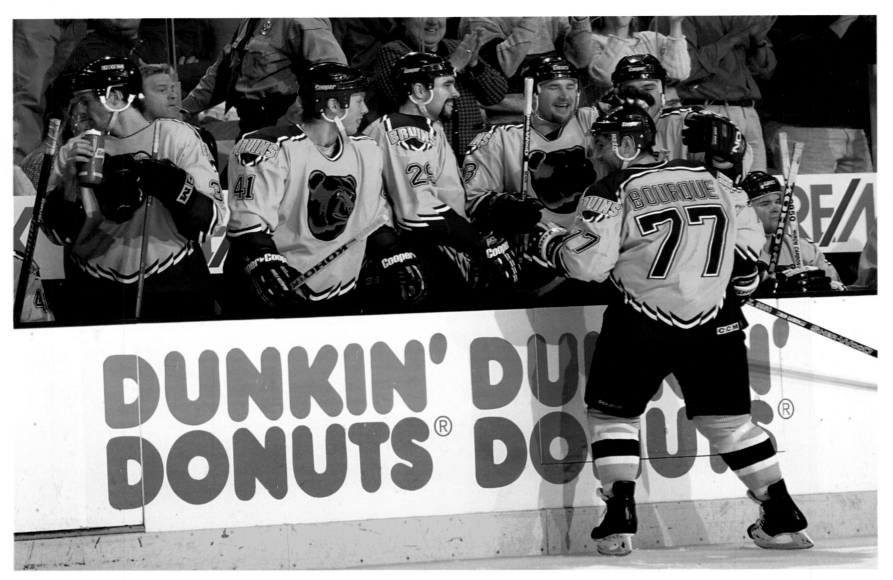

Top

PUMP IT UP!   3rd Period

*Ray Bourque rallies his troops at the bench. The momentum at this point seemed
to have swung clearly in favor of the Bruins. After giving up three unanswered
goals, they came back to tie the game on the strength of Steve Heinze's hat trick.
Then, Bourque scored on a power play to make the score 4-3, and it looked like
the game was clearly in the Bruins hands.*

Damian Strohmeyer

Previous pages

GO-AHEAD GOAL   3rd Period

*The Bruins erupt after Bourque's goal. It's announced as his 1,300th career
point but scorekeepers later give Bourque an assist on an earlier goal,
making this goal officially point no. 1,301.*

Steve Babineau

Above

TIEBREAKER   3rd Period

*Moments after Bourque's goal, Messier responds with one of his own to tie the game
4-4. Then, at 12:22 of the third period, barely two minutes after assisting on
Messier's goal, Alexei Kovalev scores the game winner with his 20th goal of the season.
In 1991, Kovalev was the first Soviet player ever taken in the first round (15th
overall) of the NHL Entry Draft.*

Damian Strohmeyer

Steve Babineau

Damian Strohmeyer

Left and above

CELEBRATION! *3rd Period*

Rangers players and fans celebrate impending victory following Kovalev's goal. Of the 567 games played between the Rangers and the Bruins to date, Rangers have won 214, Bruins have won 259 and 94 games were tied. Tonight, it's the Rangers' turn. The game's result leaves them both still in the playoff hunt, but at different ends of the spectrum: the Rangers battling with the Penguins for first place in the Eastern Conference, the Bruins struggling to stay ahead of Tampa Bay for the last playoff berth.

Return to the Windy City

Travel is a fact of life in today's NHL. You rise early and take the team bus to the airport, where you cool your heels in the departure lounge, waiting for takeoff. Soon, every airport starts to look the same. You spend so much time airborne you wonder why God didn't grant you wings. You fill the hours trying to keep cribbage boards and cards from falling off those little tables that come down from the back of the seat in front of you, playing games that never seem to begin or end. You read, you autograph pictures, you push the seat back, twist and turn, and try to get comfortable enough to sleep. • You forge friendships that will bridge the years with teammates who can be gone the next day – traded to another team. For now you share a common cause, and the game ahead is the bond that holds you together. • And then suddenly, somehow, you are back home. You have a chance to reconnect with your family, hug your wife, play with your kids, meet with friends, enjoy home cooking, and play in front of your loyal, vocal hometown fans. In short, to live a normal life for a while. • On this day the Blackhawks arrive at O'Hare at noon, having left New Jersey at 10:20 a.m. following a 4-2 victory over the Devils the night before. Tomorrow they will host the Mighty Ducks at the United Center. In the interim, some will head to the training room to get further treatment of an injury or simply continue a season-long regimen. • In their day, hockey old-timers will say, shaking their heads in amazement and perhaps suppressing a derisive snort, the hockey trainer was a guy who carried Band-Aids, a styptic pencil, and a sponge to wipe away the blood before he slapped your backside and sent you back out. • Chicago Blackhawks current medical staff includes a club doctor, club dentist, head trainer, assistant trainer, strength and conditioning coach, and a massage therapist. • No training room in today's NHL would open without exercise equipment, a whirlpool, and complex, calibrated machines to measure strength, resistance, and distance between now and recovery. The decision on whether or not an injured player is ready to return is based on those results, and the feelings of the player and the group. If the player says yes and the group consensus is no, it's no. Welcome to sports medicine, 1990s. • The rigors of a season that, counting pre-season and playoffs, could stretch well past 100 games, have made the medical team a vital part of every NHL club and the search for treatment breakthroughs as important as the search for a potential draft pick. Players have come to count on the expertise in that room, knowing it can prolong or even save a career. In the training room, the game never ends.

Facing page

O'HARE INTERNATIONAL AIRPORT *12:15 pm* CST

By late season, life on the road often seems like one big moving sidewalk. Coming back home is a welcome relief, with the prospect of rejoining friends and loved ones. Here, Chicago Blackhawks Bob Probert (left) and Joe Murphy (right) return, arriving on a flight from Newark International Airport, the day after a 4-2 Friday night victory over the New Jersey Devils.

Richard Bell

Blackhawks await takeoff in the airport departure lounge. Above: Gary Suter reads the account of Friday's game in the morning paper. Suter is the go-to guy on the Chicago power play, his hard shot from the point striking fear into goalies around the league. In last night's game against the Devils, he scored a power play marker that proved to be the winning goal. Right: Rehabilitation of an injury cannot be put off. In the Newark lounge, head trainer Mike Gapski treats Chris Chelios's injured elbow. Players around the league know that part of Chelios's anatomy all too well, as the 'Hawks defenseman has a well-deserved reputation as a physical player. But Chelios also possesses great skill at both ends of the rink, and a greater maturity has come with his assumption of the 'Hawks captaincy. He entered this, his 13th NHL season, with 600 points, and has added another 63 points, including seven power play goals, and is plus 22.

Richard Bell

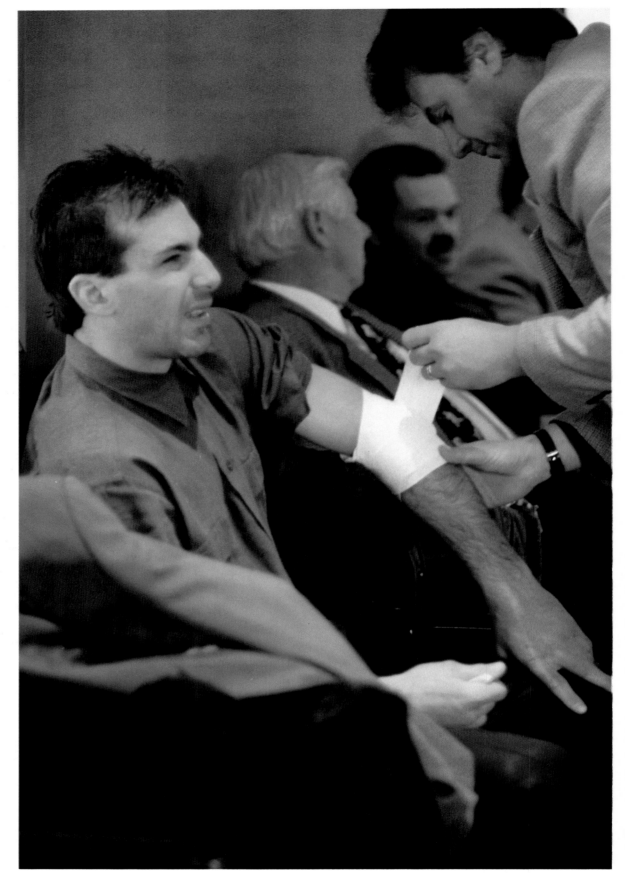

*High above the eastern United States aboard United Airlines Flight no. 645,
the Blackhawks amuse themselves, good-spirited and homeward bound.*
Above: *In his 15th NHL season, after playing 1,004 regular-season games,
Bernie Nicholls is still absorbed in the competitive aspect of his sport, in how
his team stacks up against the others. In flight, he catches up on the latest
changes in the standings. Chicago stands second in the Central Division, well
ahead of third-place St. Louis, but well back of first-place Detroit. Assured of
home ice advantage to start the playoffs, the 'Hawks could easily just run out
the string of remaining games, and look ahead to the post-season. Complacency,
however, has its hazards, and coaches and players must take care to retain
their intensity to carry a winning momentum forward into the playoffs.*
Left: *Blackhawks trainer Mike Gapski (left) and goaltender Jeff Hackett
enjoy one in a seemingly endless succession of in-flight cribbage games.*

Richard Bell

Top: *Players review a game video in the comfort of their home locker room. Chris Chelios's sons, Dean and Jake, and daughter, Kaley, join the crowd.*
Center: *Chelios roughhouses with his kids, while an injured Tony Amonte looks on. Chelios, the 'Hawks captain, is a natural leader in the dressing room and on the ice, where he has twice won the Norris Trophy for the league's best defenseman, and been voted to the First All-Star Team three times.*
Bottom: *The medical room is a busy place on the day after a game. Jeremy Roenick, leaning on a crutch to take the weight off his sprained right ankle, commiserates with Tony Amonte. If they hope to advance in the coming playoffs, the 'Hawks will need to have Roenick, their leading scorer at this point in the season, healthy and productive. Despite being hampered by injury, Roenick leads the team with 32 goals and 67 points. It's a far cry from his three-straight 100-plus point seasons in 1991-92 through '93-94, but "J.R." is still the man the 'Hawks look to for scoring when it counts.*

Richard Bell

Facing page

The Blackhawk insignia is emblematic of a rich tradition. One of the NHL's "Original Six" franchises, dating back to 1926, Chicago teams have produced many players now enshrined in the Hockey Hall of Fame. Equipment manager Troy Parchman and his staff unload players' equipment.

Richard Bell

SIGN HERE PLEASE   *1:45 pm* **CST**

*A couple of determined fans approach Jeremy Roenick for
an autograph on the concourse below the stands.*

Richard Bell

AIR MILES TO BIKE MILES   *1:50 pm* **CST**

*Mike Prokopek and James Black limber up on exercise
bicycles in the training room.*

Richard Bell

Image labels: RIC WEINRICH, GARY SUTER, CHRIS CHELIOS, JAMES B ACK

Familiarity helps players cope with the constant upheavals in their lives that are part of the season-long swings across the continent, from home stand to road trip, and back again. Players want to have their equipment laid out for them just so, the way they like it, so they can slip into their work clothes unconsciously, effortlessly, and keep their minds focused on the game ahead. Only once in the past half-century have the 'Hawks won the Stanley Cup. That was in 1961, when a team laden with legends such as Bobby Hull, Stan Mikita, goalie Glenn Hall, Elmer "Moose" Vasko, and Pierre Pilote beat Gordie Howe and the Detroit Red Wings four games to two. In recent years, Chicago has shown signs of attaining championship form, especially in 1991-92 when, on the strength of a 53-goal season by Jeremy Roenick, and standout playoff goal-tending from Ed Belfour, they made it to the Stanley Cup final, only to fall to the Penguins in four games. This season, they have flirted with the top five overall rankings in the league, raising hopes and dreams among Blackhawk fans of that long-awaited Cup victory.

Richard Bell

The Long, Hard Road

A marker board is attached to the wall behind Mike Milbury's desk in the coaches' office at Nassau Coliseum. Milbury, first-season coach and general manager of the New York Islanders, wants people cheering in their seats at the arena as they used to cheer Bob Nystrom, Denis Potvin, Mike Bossy, and Billy Smith when the Islanders won four consecutive Stanley Cups starting in 1980. At this point in this season, however, his team has already fallen completely out of playoff contention. His work, this game day, is to make sure his Islanders will be in the playoffs, or much closer to them, when next April comes around. ● The board bears the outline of a hockey rink and Milbury, marker in hand, becomes an artist at the canvas. "I'm excited. I really am," he says. "Here's why. I'll tell you why." He writes Eric Fichaud's name. "This kid's playing better every game," Milbury says of the 20-year-old goaltender. "Why wouldn't I be excited? He's just getting started." He writes Kenny Jonsson's name. "He's going to be a terrific player," Milbury says of the 21-year-old defenseman. "He just needs to get stronger." He writes defenseman Bryan McCabe's name. "This kid, he's the same. He gives you everything, every night." Then another defenseman, Darius Kasparaitis. "He's one of the most hated players in the league, and he just loves to play," Milbury says of the 23-year-old Lithuanian. "If you're putting in excitement, you put Bryan Berard's name there." He shifts to the forwards, writes the name of Todd Bertuzzi, a six-foot-three rookie right-winger with wonderful hands. "This kid is coming on. Incredible offensive skills," Milbury says, continuing to write. The marker becomes a black blur, the hockey rink vanishing under all the names. Bertuzzi, Ziggy Palffy, Travis Green. A nice first line. Milbury leaves a gap on the board for the second and third lines, positions he will try to fill – or fill better – over the summer. ● But this night, the Islanders will have to make do with what they have, and it's not enough. New Jersey's Steve Thomas, ironically an Islander until last season, scores to break a 2-2 tie in overtime, and a sold-out crowd goes home miserable. For Devils head coach Jacques Lemaire, it's one positive step in a season that has had all too few bright spots. Especially for the defending Stanley Cup champions. Especially for Lemaire, so used to winning as a Hall of Fame player with the Canadiens. ● For Milbury, it was wrenching and reassuring, at the same time, to have all the day's planning and all the day's work end in defeat. "You know what's coming, but you know you don't have enough now," says Milbury, rumpled and drained – near tears. "It was a good day for a guy who wanted to see his team play that way. It was just a tough day for the team that worked as hard as it did and executed the game plan for the most part and didn't win." ● A good day, a bad result. "Yeah. And that stinks. Doesn't it? It does," Milbury says. "It hurts. It hurts. I haven't had a loss like this one in a good long time. I thought we had them. I felt like we were going to make a statement. And we did, because we played our hearts out. We just weren't good enough." Maybe, some day, they will be, when Milbury fills in those blanks on his drawing board.

Facing page

Subway Series   *1st Period*

In their final meeting of the season, rivals New Jersey Devils and New York Islanders contend for New York City commuter-belt bragging rights. Here, Devils Jason Smith keeps Islanders Pat Flatley away from his goalie, Martin Brodeur. The Islanders are a rebuilding franchise. The Devils, last year's Stanley Cup victors, are struggling to repeat.

Brian Winkler/BBS

On this game day, Islanders hold a light morning practice session.
Top left: *In a relaxed moment before practice begins, Islanders general manager and coach Mike Milbury skates with his 14-year-old daughter, Alison. A veteran of 21 professional seasons as a player, coach, assistant general manager, and broadcaster, Milbury – since relieving Don Maloney earlier this season – has added general manager to his resume. His primary task is to rebuild the Islanders from the bottom up. Bottom left: The word best applied to Pat Flatley's style of play is "commitment." It's an all-out, self-sacrificing dedication to winning that has caused him to miss many games throughout his 13-year career, giving up his body to make the check, to take the hit that will spring a teammate for a scoring chance. But winning has not come easily to the Islanders this season, and, as their captain, Flatley feels the weight of their ill fortune.*

Paul Bereswill

Top right: *For a while this afternoon, the New York Islanders former glory is relived in a game between Islanders alumni and the Wall Street Hockey Team, a pick-up assemblage of stockbrokers. Right-winger Bob Nystrom (far right) saw his name inscribed on the Stanley Cup four straight years, from 1979-80 through 1982-83. Here, as he surveys the bench, many of the faces he sees are those who played with him on Cup-winning teams: Gord Lane and Jean Potvin, among others. Ed Westfall (center), two-time Stanley Cup winner who started his career with the Boston Bruins and finished with the Islanders in '78-79, takes a breather from the on-ice action. Bottom right: In a conference held in the coaches' room two hours before game time, Islanders assistant coach Guy Charron diagrams a play, while associate coach Rick Bowness (left) and coach and general manager Mike Milbury look on. Together, they offer the Islanders one of the more experienced coaching combinations in the league. All three have served as head coach with other teams: Milbury with the Boston Bruins, Bowness with the Bruins and Ottawa Senators, and Charron, on an interim basis, with the Calgary Flames.*

Paul Bereswill

Autograph-seeking fans snag Devils players as they approach the arena on their way to prepare for tonight's game. With 11 games left in the regular season, the Islanders have long been eliminated from post-season play. For the Devils, more is at stake, as the defending Stanley Cup Champions are struggling to keep their playoff hopes alive. One of the few positives for the Devils this season has been the play of goaltender Martin Brodeur. Calder Trophy winner as the NHL's top rookie in 1993-94 and outstanding in New Jersey's Stanley Cup triumph last year, Brodeur has kept himself in the top five in the league in save percentage and goals against despite the inconsistent play in front of him.

Barton Silverman

WARM-UP

Pre-game

Above: *As fans settle into their seats in the arena, both teams conduct their warm-ups, loosening up their muscles and working out their pre-game jitters, as the time approaches for the first puck to be dropped.* Right: *On behalf of his team, Islanders veteran captain Pat Flatley presents a check to the Leukemia Society in the amount of $7,500. The money was raised through NHL SuperSkills, a league-wide program to showcase players' abilities, culminating in a head-to-head competition at the annual All-Star Weekend. The spirit of giving something back to the community is strong in the NHL, with players and teams participating in a wide range of charitable causes and fundraising events.*

GAME ON

1st Period

*The first puck is dropped, and the teams skate to a scoreless first period.
Islanders rugged defenseman Darius Kasparaitis ties up Devils right-winger
Stéphane Richer along the boards, under the watchful eye of referee Dave
Jackson. A 1-0 Islanders lead on Zigmund Palffy's goal, just 54 seconds into
the second period, holds up until Devils center Bobby Holik responds at
3:56 of the third with his 10th.*

Paul Bereswill

COMMISSIONER BETTMAN

1st Period

*High above ice level, National Hockey League Commissioner Gary Bettman and
his wife Shelli survey the game. Under Bettman's leadership, the League has
expanded to new markets, introducing new fans to the excitement of NHL hockey
throughout North America.*

Barton Silverman

Once the game begins, Bob Nystrom (right) dons his street clothes and climbs upstairs to the broadcast booth, where he joins play-by-play announcer Barry Landers (to Nystrom's right) to give color commentary for the Islanders' radio broadcast.

Barton Silverman

Devils give back as good as they get. Here, left-winger Valeri Zelepukin takes his opposite number, Dan Plante, out of the play. A native of Voskresensk in Russia, Zelepukin is in his fifth year with the Devils. Still on the rebound from an injury-riddled 1994-95 season, this season he has yet to regain the form that made him a consistent 20-plus goal contributor in 1992-93 and '93-94.

Paul Bereswill

As the game's intensity rises, players on the the Islanders bench lean forward to follow the play. For the second time in the game, Islanders take the lead, this time on Alexander Semak's 20th goal of the season. The Devils draw even on Stéphane Richer's 10th. In the last five minutes of regulation time, both the Islanders and Devils have good chances to score the game-winner, but the horn blows at the end of the third period with the two teams deadlocked 2-2.

Paul Bereswill

Above

ROOKIE VS ROOKIE   *Overtime*

*As overtime begins, the Devils press hard. Devils rookie center Steve Sullivan
drifts the puck across the open goal mouth behind Islanders rookie goaltender Eric Fichaud. Both are recent arrivals with their respective teams.
In just his 11th game after being called up from the Albany River Rats,
New Jersey's American Hockey League affiliate, Sullivan has four
goals and two assists. Fichaud, a 1994 first-round draft pick of the
Maple Leafs, traded late last season in exchange for Benoit Hogue, is
starting just his 15th game tonight, having spent part of the season
with the Worcester Icecats of the AHL.*

Paul Bereswill

Following pages

GAME WINNER   *Overtime*

*Then, the breakthrough. At 3:38 of the overtime period, right-winger Steve
Thomas puts the puck behind a sprawling Fichaud. Against his former team,
he scores his sixth game-winning goal of the season.*

Paul Bereswill

Top: *Alone at the other end of the rink, Devils goalie Martin
Brodeur jumps for joy as Steve Thomas scores the winner.*
Bottom: *Thomas is embraced by teammate Bill Guerin, who
assisted on the winning goal, as the victorious Devils skate off
the ice. For tonight at least, they are still on the playoff hunt.*

A STUDY IN CONTRASTS   *Post-game*

All the responsibility, and little of the glory, goes to the head coaches. Top: *In the Islanders dressing room, Mike Milbury sags, knowing that his team gave their best effort, but still fell short.* Bottom: *Tired but confident, Jacques Lemaire pauses on his way out of the arena to give one last autograph.*

Mister Consistency

In an era where young millionaire players are granted more and more freedom – or so goes the conventional wisdom of the nineties – coaching has become a young man's game, thirty-something communicators who haven't forgotten what it was like to be 20; coaching minds uncluttered by old-school thinking. • Scotty Bowman must find that amusing, staring down at his six Stanley Cup rings, looking back on a quarter-century as an NHL head coach, watching his "Russian Five" flash around the ice in practice – a symbol of the most daring step taken by any team this season. • It wasn't one of the new wave of coaches who dared to take five Russian players, put them in a unit and say, "Okay, go out and do what you do." It was William Scott Bowman, who turns 63 in September. Bowman has taken four different teams to the Stanley Cup final and on this day is odds-on favorite to take the Detroit Red Wings back again to avenge last season's embarrassment at the hands of the New Jersey Devils. • Thirty-something? Try 900-something, as in the number of regular season victories for teams coached by a man already in the Hockey Hall of Fame, and still very much at the top of his game. • When the NHL doubled its size in 1967-68, Bowman was there – a rookie head coach who took the St. Louis Blues to the Cup final for three straight years. Twenty-nine seasons later here he sits, coach and director of player personnel for his fifth NHL team. In between: legendary years with the Montreal Canadiens. Result: four straight Stanley Cups from 1976 to 1979. Then building years in Buffalo and Pittsburgh, where he came down from the executive suite when illness felled Penguins head coach Bob Johnson. Result: a Stanley Cup in 1992 to go with the one he helped orchestrate as director of player development and recruitment in 1991. • Bowman doesn't worry about eras or fads or fashions in coaching; he ignores them. And no one does a better job of cutting his suit to fit his cloth. • This season he looked at the strong Russian content on his club – a certified NHL superstar in winger Sergei Fedorov, Hart Trophy winner in 1993-94; on the other wing, Vyacheslav Kozlov, a member of Russian World Championship teams in 1991 and 1994; a rock-solid defense with Vladimir Konstantinov and the aging-but-wily Slava Fetisov – and asked himself a question: What would happen if he got a Russian center who knew these players, and let them all play as a unit in the Russian system they'd been steeped in since birth? Then he went out and traded to get Igor Larionov, center of the famed KLM Line in the legendary years of Soviet hockey, who was languishing in San Jose. Young coaches might have thought of that, but would they have dared to try it? Scotty Bowman just smiles and does his own thing. If another wave of the future comes along, chances are he'll ride that one, too.

Facing page

CERTIFIED WINNER   *2:00 pm* **EST**

Seven times Scott Bowman's name has been inscribed on the Stanley Cup. Six times players he has coached have had their names entered in the record books as champions. Will this be another? Bowman, with 968 wins and counting, is the all-time winningest NHL coach. He has led the Red Wings to the best record in hockey the past two seasons, with but one goal remaining: to bring the Wings to their first Stanley Cup in more than four decades.

Grant Black

Top		Bottom	
RED WINGS LOCKER ROOM	*1:15 pm* **EST**	PRACTICE MAKES PERFECT	*2:00 pm* **EST**

Dressing for on-ice action follows a ritual: first come the undergarments, then the pads, last, players lace up their skates, and don their jerseys, assuming their team identity. The modern-day warrior's suit of armor is complete. Left to right: Kris Draper, Sergei Fedorov, and Darren McCarty.

William Strode

Even the NHL's elite practice the skills and drills that are the basic building blocks of the game. This includes the Detroit Red Wings, who take advantage of an off-day to hone their technique. Strong fundamentals allow players to react to game situations spontaneously and automatically, at the break-neck pace set by the world's best hockey players.

William Strode

Top left: *The defensive pairing of perennial All-Star Paul Coffey (left) and Nicklas Lidstrom is one of the most effective in the league. Including last night's game against Colorado, Coffey has 58 points on the season, and Lidstrom 59.* Bottom left: *Scotty Bowman's bold experiment of putting five Russian players, schooled in the system that brought the Soviets international gold so often, on the ice at one time has paid off magnificently. The three forwards – Sergei Fedorov, Igor Larionov, and Vyacheslav Kozlov – have each scored over 30 goals so far, and defenseman Vladimir Konstantinov leads the league in plus-minus, while the other defenseman, Viacheslav Fetisov, also ranks in the top five plus-minus league-wide. Left to right: Fedorov, Konstantinov, Fetisov, and Larionov.*

William Strode

Top right: *After practice, players take time to stop on their way down the tunnel to the locker room and chat with their loyal hometown fans. Here, Sergei Fedorov and Martin Lapointe respond to requests for autographs.* Bottom right: *Bob Errey laces up a skate for his son, Conor, who joined his father after practice. Errey, former captain of the San Jose Sharks, adds character to a dressing room laden with talent. And he's enjoying being reunited with his linemate from junior hockey's Peterborough Petes, Red Wings captain Steve Yzerman. Ironically, although Yzerman has had the headlines – including scoring his 500th career goal earlier this season – it is Errey who wears two Stanley Cup rings, from 1990-91 and '91-92 with the Pittsburgh Penguins.*

William Strode

Goalie Mike Vernon strides by the stick rack on his way off the ice. On the wall above hang plaques bearing the names of Red Wings notables from yesteryear. For the players, it is a constant reminder of past glory – but also a nagging admonition to make the most of their current predominance: no Wings team has won the Cup since the 1954-55 season.

William Strode

Top

AFTER PRACTICE   2:55 pm EST

To the player, media requests for interviews are part of the daily routine. Here, while the locker room clears as players head for the airport for their flight to St. Louis, Steve Yzerman grants one last reporter's request, this one from Viv Bernstein of the Detroit Free Press. This year, "Stevie Y" reached a milestone few NHLers surpass: the 500-goal plateau. As of Friday's game against Colorado, his career totals are 517 goals, 1,246 assists. Now, as his 13th NHL season comes to a close, the Red Wings captain may wonder if this is the year he will enjoy one achievement he has so far been denied: Stanley Cup victory.

William Strode

Above

READY TO TRAVEL   3:05 pm EST

All dressed up with nowhere to go but the top. In a handful of years in the league, Sergei Fedorov has established himself as a superior talent. He won both the Hart and Selke Trophies after the 1993-94 season. At this point in this season he leads the Red Wings in scoring, and his +39 plus-minus rating is second only to that of teammate Vladimir Konstantinov overall in the league.

William Strode

Following pages

OAKLAND-PONTIAC AIRPORT   4:25 pm EST

Fifty minutes' drive north of Detroit, the Red Wings board their private jet, a BAC-111, which seats 40 in considerable comfort. An hour and a half after takeoff, they will touch down at Cahokia Airport, just outside St. Louis, on the way to a Sunday contest against the Blues. Viacheslav Fetisov mounts the stairs.

William Strode

The New Breed

So it has come to this in the NHL: A coach can be your pal, your golfing buddy, even a former roommate. That's the relationship between Paul Maurice, head coach of the Hartford Whalers, and Glen Featherstone, Whaler defenseman. It's all part of a shift toward younger coaches in pro sports, who some have called the "new breed." ● Maurice, hired at age 28, takes that trend to an extreme. His counterpart on the evening of March 23, Jim Schoenfeld of the Washington Capitals, also fits that description, from his boyish appearance to his playful banter with his players to his willingness to listen, really listen, to their ideas. Is the difference in approach a question of age or of attitude? ● There are still "old style" coaches in the NHL, most prominently Detroit's Scotty Bowman, St. Louis's Mike Keenan, and New Jersey's Jacques Lemaire. And, they're still successful, all three having coached recent Stanley Cup winners. Steve Kasper, at 34 the second youngest head coach in the NHL, took a staunch approach when he benched two of his high-priced Boston Bruins, Cam Neely and Kevin Stevens, for a game this season. He put them in uniform, put them on the bench, and left them there. ● Maurice's situation – half the team are his age or older – was a cause for apprehension when he replaced the fired Paul Holmgren early this season. Quickly, though, the Whalers sensed that Maurice "has the maturity like those older coaches, but he understands what it's like to be our age," Featherstone says. Still, it's a fine line that Maurice walks. "They don't stop telling stories too much when I walk in the room," he says, "but you don't want them telling a story about being out after curfew." ● Jim Schoenfeld, too, is not a taskmaster. Oh, he yells when he feels he has to, but he'll also joke with the guys at the rink and on the bus. More important, he listens to them. Once last season, when the Capitals trailed the Philadelphia Flyers by a goal with 13.4 seconds left, Schoenfeld called a time-out and set up a play. But veteran Michal Pivonka, who was to take the face-off, suggested a change. Schoenfeld agreed – and the Capitals scored 2.5 seconds after the face-off. "For me not to listen to any player would be arrogant at the least and foolish at the worst," says Schoenfeld. "Now, whether I take their suggestion and implement it is entirely different. I think you always have to listen because you never know where the next great idea is coming from." ● So perhaps it is an oversimplification, referring to today's coaches as the "new breed." "I really don't think there's a new breed of coaches," Schoenfeld says. "Coaching to me is an ever-learning job. Sometimes the learning brings you right back to the old method. It's not like every day or every new coaching generation you get new coaching revelations. Sometimes it's a matter of just a little twist on the old way of doing things – and sometimes it's going right back to the old way of doing things. Coaches, though, always have to be open to new ideas."

CENTER OF ATTENTION   *3rd Period*

Action swirls around Capitals stellar goal-tender, Jim Carey, as his teammates Michal Pivonka (left) and Sergei Gonchar try to clear Whalers Robert Kron out of the crease. March has been an outstanding month in each of Carey's two NHL seasons. Last year, he was voted Player of the Month, a rarity for a rookie. This year, he is a strong candidate to repeat the honor, coming into tonight's game having recorded three shutouts since March 1.

Jerry Wachter

Top

CAPITALS COACHES ROOM   *10:00 am* **EST**

Capitals head coach Jim Schoenfeld fields reporters' questions during game day interviews. Under Schoenfeld, in his second full season at the helm, the Capitals currently rank in the top 10 teams in the NHL. Recently, he took his team to task in the media, blaming some players for their deficient work ethic. The Capitals responded with two straight winning performances. Using the media to issue a public challenge to his own players may seem a risky venture, but it's indicative of Schoenfeld's innovative approach to coaching.

Bruce Bennett

Above

CAPITALS LOCKER ROOM   *10:00 am* **EST**

Stretching out the kinks before practice ensures goaltender Jim Carey's legs will have the flexibility crucial to survive the acrobatic moves in the goal crease needed in a practice or game situation.

Bruce Bennett

The locker room becomes a second home for players. It's a place where they spend a good part of their professional life. Individually, they can focus on making their bodies strong, to endure the gruelling pace of NHL hockey. Together, they can bond to create the camaraderie and team spirit that are essential ingredients of a winner. Above: *During the season, as well as in the summer months, players ride miles on the stationary bicycle. Aerobic conditioning and leg strength are fundamental to maintaining physical stamina over the long NHL season. Here, defenseman Ken Klee, out with a strained groin, focuses on his rehabilitation.* Left: *Defensive-minded defenseman Joe Reekie shares a joke with trainer Doug Shearer. Some players stay loose as game time approaches. Others stay quiet and focus on their own thoughts.*

Bruce Bennett

THE WHALER NEWS   11:00 am EST

Keeping abreast of your team's place in the standings
becomes important at this point in the season. On the bus
from their hotel, the Greenbelt Marriott, to the USAir
Arena for an optional skate, (from left) Brian Glynn,
Brad McCrimmon, and Sean Burke catch up on news-
paper accounts of last night's game – a 1-1 tie with
the Senators in Ottawa.

Annie Griffiths Belt

THE SPORTS PAGE   11:15 am EST

The players aren't the only ones who closely follow the
fortunes of the team. Whalers equipment manager Wally
Tatomir takes a break from his chores in the visitors' locker
room at the USAir Arena to read the overnight results.
Whalers chances for post-season play are receding rapidly.

Annie Griffiths Belt

Top

OPTIONAL PRACTICE   *11:15 am* EST

Goaltender Sean Burke has been between the pipes for 25 of the Whalers 30 wins so far this season, including three shutouts, both career highs. Burke tended goal for the Canadian Olympic Team in 1988, and in 1992, when they won a silver medal at Albertville.

Annie Griffiths Belt

Bottom

NAP TIME   *1:30 pm* EST

Back at the hotel for a pre-game nap, Scott Daniels makes a brief call home while his roommate, Whalers captain Brendan Shanahan, cruises the TV dial. Daniels is making the most of learning the craft of playing left wing from Shanahan, one of the best power forwards in the game.

Annie Griffiths Belt

Preparing for game after game, year in year out, players fall into certain patterns of behavior. Some are functional, while others border on superstition. Top: *Whalers left-winger Geoff Sanderson heats his stick blade in pursuit of the perfect curve.* Center: *For an offensive defenseman like Jeff Brown, a mid-season arrival from the Vancouver Canucks, customizing sticks is an important pre-game ritual. Since coming to Hartford, Brown has taken control of the Whalers power play, directing action from the left point.* Bottom: *Capitals assistant captain Kelly Miller sits in the stands before every game, dressed in his street clothes, visualizing the action to come. He is one of the premier defensive forwards in the league, and his dedication and commitment, game after game, are a model for others.*

Annie Griffiths Belt

Annie Griffiths Belt

Previous Pages

After their pre-game nap, players arrive early at the arena for the game. Whalers medical trainer Frank "Bud" Gouveia tapes Kevin Dineen's healing right wrist. Hartford has missed the veteran leadership of Dineen, who was with the Whalers from 1984 until traded to the Flyers in 1991. Before he was reacquired December 28, Hartford was 11-19-5, but after his arrival, team fortunes improved to 12-6-1 until his injury. Since then, they have again fallen below .500. In the background, defensemen Gerald Diduck (left) and Brian Glynn discuss their aches and pains with team massage therapist David Duffy (standing).

Annie Griffiths Belt

Bruce Bennett

THE BLUES   Game End

His face a study in frustration, Nelson Emerson (left) leaves the ice with his captain, Shanahan. Former teammates with the St. Louis Blues, now reunited, both are fierce competitors. The Whalers have let another win slip away. Up 2-1 on a late-second-period goal by Shanahan, the team was counting on a win. The one point they gain for a tie is cold comfort at this point in the Whalers season, when every lost opportunity puts them one step closer to playoff elimination.

Annie Griffiths Belt

DRAWING EVEN   3rd Period

Midway through the third period, Peter Bondra lifts the puck over Burke's out-stretched right leg to tie the game 2-2, and that's how it ended. At 41 goals, the Capitals high flying right-winger has already surpassed his career best total. With 11 regular-season games remaining, Bondra is on pace to break 50. A large part of the credit for Bondra's goal production goes to his selfless center, Michal Pivonka, who, as he does on this goal, sets Bondra up with perfect passes.

Jerry Wachter

Reaching Altitude

At face value, the 1995-96 season may be the inaugural year of the Colorado Avalanche, but it's really a year of culmination for two great hockey traditions. • For the city of Denver, its association with professional hockey hails back to 1950 and the Denver Falcons of the short-lived United States Hockey League. In the intervening years, a succession of pro hockey franchises has made the Colorado capital their home. With names like Mavericks, Invaders, Spurs, Flames, Rangers, Rockies, and Grizzlies, teams had their day in the sun and the snow, and then moved on. • Franchises may have come and gone, but their cumulative effect was to build a strong constituency for hockey in the state of Colorado. When the call went out on June 21, 1995, that a new NHL franchise was coming to Denver, 12,000 season tickets were sold within 37 days. • But then, this was no ordinary first-year franchise. As the Quebec Nordiques, it was one of four former World Hockey Association teams that joined the National Hockey League for the 1979 season. In their early NHL years, the Nordiques did not lack for stellar players, starting with Michel Goulet, their first pick in the 1979 entry draft, and Peter Stastny, winner of the Calder Trophy in 1981. • But by the late eighties and early nineties the team had stalled, finishing out of playoff contention or bowing out in the early rounds. Since then, the team has turned itself around, and finished the 1994-95 season with the second best record in the NHL. • The transformation has followed the very different fates of three players. One of them, Eric Lindros, never played a game for the franchise. Chosen by the Nordiques first overall in 1991, he refused to report. One year later, he was traded to Philadelphia for six players, three of whom – Peter Forsberg, Mike Ricci, and Chris Simon – are still impact players with the team. • A throw-in with the Lindros deal was a couple of Flyer draft choices. The resulting pick in 1993 was goaltender Jocelyn Thibault. He became the goalie who went the other way when a daring trade in the fall of 1995 brought another key piece of the puzzle – restless two-time Stanley Cup netminder Patrick Roy – to the Avalanche from the Montreal Canadiens. • The third key, especially this season, has been the strong play and leadership of Colorado captain Joe Sakic, a first-round draft pick in 1987 who has blossomed into one of the league's top scorers. Brought together, the pieces of the puzzle have clicked into place in 1995-96. At this point in the season, they have already clinched a playoff berth. In the entire NHL, only the Detroit Red Wings have more points. • And Colorado hockey fans now have a team that's here to stay. In a land of snow and an abundance of natural energy, the game of hockey is a sure fit. When the NHL arrived in the form of the Avalanche, with the Bigfoot crest on their shoulders, it was love at first sight.

Facing page

NEAR TOUCHDOWN   *4:45 pm* **CST**

Through eight seasons with this franchise, Curtis Leschyshyn has logged a lot of air miles. His fortunes have followed his team's, which have gone from worst to first. This year, they are second only to Detroit overall, and Leschyshyn remains one of their most dependable defensemen. Like his rookie-year roommate, Joe Sakic, he is hoping that this season their trials and tribulations will be rewarded.

Grant Black

CITY SPORTS CENTER, DETROIT   *11:00 am* EST

*Proud of his heritage, hard-rock left-winger Chris Simon
is a role model for Native youth aspiring to make it in the
NHL – and in life. Prior to his team's practice, Simon
hosts a televised skate with three young players from the
Six Nations Reserve near Brantford, Ontario.*

Grant Black

THE SPARK   *11:30 am* EST

*Avalanche management are hoping Claude Lemieux – a
spur to his team and a burr in the side of his opponents –
last year's Conn Smythe winner as a New Jersey Devil,
can show his new teammates how to win the big one.*

Grant Black

The morning after an embarrassing 7-0 loss to the league-leading Red Wings, the Avalanche endure a brutal workout. Top left: Head coach Marc Crawford lays down the law for his players. Last year's NHL Coach of the Year will settle for nothing less than this year's Stanley Cup. Top right: Sakic (left) and defenseman Curtis Leschyshyn pay heed. Detroit is the only team in the Western Conference with a better record than Colorado, and the Avalanche must surely get by them to make it to the Finals. Bottom left: In 1993 goaltender Patrick Roy led the Canadiens to the Cup. The question on the lips of hockey fans in Denver is: "Can he do the same this year for the Avalanche?" Bottom right: Sometimes travel brings NHL players closer to their families. A visit to Detroit means veteran defenseman Craig Wolanin – who hails from nearby Grosse Pointe, Michigan – can visit with his four-year-old niece, Kate.

Grant Black

Weary after their workout, players trudge up the staircase onto the charter that will take them to Winnipeg, site of tomorrow afternoon's game against the Jets, another franchise on the move. It will be the Avalanche's last regular-season visit to the Manitoba capital. The team normally travels in their comfortably equipped team plane, but a minor mechanical delay today has left it grounded.

Grant Black

Spirits lift as the plane takes off – and the food comes out. Jean Martineau (left), director of media relations and team services, shares a joke with players. It was not just the players who moved house last year. Many of the management and staff – such as Martineau, who has been with the franchise nine years – came to Colorado with the franchise.

Grant Black

On the road, an NHL team's training staff works round-the-clock, doing whatever it takes to make the team's equipment ready for the next game. They cannot rest until every player's needs are catered to, and all their tools of the trade are checked and repaired or polished, then safely stowed. Here, his day's work not done, but over for a moment, assistant equipment manager Mike Kramer snoozes under a good book.

Grant Black

WINNIPEG 5:45 pm **CST**

Journey's end – for today, at least. Undeterred by a piercingly cold winter wind and sub-zero temperatures, a clutch of hardy autograph seekers approaches the players as they step off the bus from the airport. For Curtis Leschyshyn (on steps), from northern Manitoba, this will be his last chance to play before a home-town crowd. A serious knee injury in 1991 made him think about retiring. He chose to stick it out and work hard on his rehabilitation. Was it worth it? The outcome of this season will tell.

Grant Black

Above

HEADING FOR HEAT 5:50 pm **CST**

Patrick Roy grants one last fan's request as he strides toward his hotel. When, in a blockbuster pre-Christmas trade, the Montreal Canadiens traded their star goaltender to Colorado, Avalanche fans were elated. They hoped Roy, three-time winner of the Vezina Trophy as the league's best goaltender, would be the guide to lead them to the peak. It was clear that, as Conn Smythe Trophy winner in 1986 and 1993, Roy knew the way.

Grant Black

The Ghosts of the Forum

The smell of fresh paint is in the air. There's an anticipatory look on fans' faces as they try to navigate their way through new corridors to their seats. They have come to watch the Canadiens play the Oilers, but they are also here to experience the newest arena in the NHL. The Molson Centre is part of a trend. Since 1993, new arenas have been built in Anaheim, Boston, Chicago, Ottawa, St. Louis, San Jose, and Vancouver. New establishments in Buffalo, Philadelphia, and Tampa Bay will open in time for the 1996-97 season. ● The Canadiens left behind a shrine when they moved from the Forum, but there are two areas in the Molson Centre that bear a striking resemblance to the historic arena. The first is under the rafters, where 31 banners hang, commemorating the record 24 Stanley Cups won by the Canadiens and the seven retired jersey numbers of Jacques Plante, Jean Beliveau, Doug Harvey, Howie Morenz, Guy Lafleur, and the Richard brothers, Maurice and Henri. ● Eight stories below, at ice level, is the second: As the Canadiens prepare for tonight's game against the Edmonton Oilers, they see around them, on the walls of their new locker room, the faces of former Habs players who are now in the Hockey Hall of Fame. Beneath the photos, just as in the old Forum, is inscribed a line from John McCrae's poem "In Flanders Fields": "To you from failing hands we throw the torch. Be yours to hold it high." ● Those words have inspired the Canadiens for more than four decades. Their meaning was brought home to the current players less than two weeks before tonight, after they played their final game at the Forum. In a stirring ceremony, the torch was indeed passed, from Emile Bouchard – the oldest living captain – to Maurice Richard and on to other former captains: Beliveau to Henri Richard to Yvan Cournoyer to Serge Savard to Bob Gainey to Guy Carbonneau and, finally, to current captain Pierre Turgeon. ● The illustrious history acted out at the legendary building on Rue Sainte-Catherine gave a sense of destiny to Montreal teams and placed a heavy burden on visitors. Friend and foe alike came to believe the Forum was inhabited by ghosts who looked favorably on the Habs. Tonight the ghosts must have been sleeping, as the Edmonton Oilers, themselves a storied NHL dynasty, skate to victory on the strength of a five-point, three-goal effort from Jason Arnott. ● Tears have been shed over the closing of the Forum – Rocket Richard had to fight to hold his back when the fans gave him a 12-minute ovation on closing night – but the tradition lives on through the wet paint and sparkling new luxury boxes. It lives on in the storied banners hanging from the rafters. It lives on in those fabled words on the dressing room wall. These words are a reminder to the current generation of young men who proudly wear the Canadiens sweater. This is a team steeped in history, and it is their task to write a new chapter, their job to give this new building a history and tradition as rich as that of the Forum.

Facing page

FLYING CHANGE　　　　　*3rd Period*

The Montreal Canadiens change lines as game action continues down ice. The franchise has just undergone the most momentous change in its history, by moving from the storied Forum, its permanent home since 1926. Tradition made it tough to leave a building that was witness to 22 Montreal Canadiens Stanley Cup winners, but in the new Molson Centre, the team has a grand venue in which it can continue its winning tradition well into a new century.

Michel Gravel

Top

HALL OF FAME HAB

9:55 am **EST**

There is no shortage of Montreal Canadiens – "les habitants" or "Habs" to their fans – represented in the Hockey Hall of Fame. Henri Richard, the "Pocket Rocket" in reference to his brother Maurice "Rocket" Richard, is one of the most widely respected. Pictured here enjoying a brilliant early spring morning on the banks of La Rivière des Prairies near his home in the Montreal suburb of Laval, Richard, in 20 seasons with the Canadiens, was a member of an NHL-record 11 Stanley Cup-winning teams.

Michel Gravel

Above

CAPTURED ON FILM

9:00 am **EST**

Covering the Montreal Canadiens for 33 seasons, photographer Denis Brodeur has frozen for posterity many historic moments in hockey. Now we turn the tables, photographing him with his wife, Mireille, cooking breakfast in their kitchen. One opposition player Denis makes sure he has in his viewfinder when New Jersey comes to town is his son Martin Brodeur, the Devils Stanley Cup-winning goaltender. Tonight, Denis will be at the Molson Centre to shoot the Oilers and Canadiens.

Tedd Church

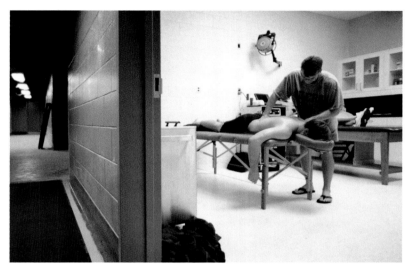

The varied day of an NHL team on the road has many faces.
Top left: *Sometimes even superstars don't get preferential treatment. Here Edmonton Oilers head coach Ron Low tears a strip off talented third-year center Jason Arnott. Bottom left: After practice, massage therapist Roland Kelly works on Doug Weight. The bumps and bruises are starting to take their toll on Weight, who is receiving more physical attention from opposing centers, since he is having a career-best year, consistently among the league's top 10 in scoring throughout the season.*

Peter Martin

Top right: *From his Montreal hotel room, Oilers long-serving director of public relations Bill Tuele keeps abreast of a myriad of details and arrangements – coordinating such things as media requests and public appearances.*
Bottom right: *Oilers goaltender Curtis Joseph browses the magazine rack in the shopping mall below the team's hotel. When the Oilers traded their no. 1 goalie Bill Ranford to Boston on January 11, they needed an experienced hand to step right in. Joseph, who had become Edmonton property in an off-season trade with St. Louis, was starring in goal with the Las Vegas Thunder of the International Hockey League. Since coming to Edmonton, the veteran of six NHL campaigns has been prominent in the Oilers last-minute drive for the playoffs.*

Peter Martin

Michel Gravel

Michel Gravel

Michel Gravel

Peter Martin

THE TRADITION CONTINUES   *Pre-game*

The quality and professionalism of the Montreal Canadiens operation has long been the envy of other franchises. Top left: *Ronald Corey, team president since 1982, who presided over the creation of the Molson Centre, brims with pride inside the just-opened structure. The Centre seats 21,450 – nearly 4,500 more than the old Forum.* Bottom left: *Pierre Bouchard, who served on the Habs blue line through five Stanley Cups from 1970 to 1978, admires a plaque bearing the visage of his Hall-of-Fame father, Emile "Butch" Bouchard, who captained the Canadiens half a century ago.*

WELL PREPARED   *Pre-game*

Top right: *Experienced ushers casually discuss the upcoming evening in the new arena.* Bottom right: *Security guard Danny DiPaolo checks his watch at 6:55 pm outside the Edmonton locker room, as the Oilers begin to stir in advance of heading out for their last-minute, pre-game skate.*

HOCKEY NIGHT IN CANADA   7:45 pm **EST**

Broadcasters Dick Irvin, Jr. (right) and Greg Millen (left) call the game from their vantage point high above the ice surface. Moving to the Molson Centre was an adjustment for Irvin, who had known the Forum since he was a child, back in the 1940s and '50s, when he watched his father, Dick Sr., coach the Montreal Canadiens.

Michel Gravel

STATING THEIR CASE   1st Period

Montreal captain Pierre Turgeon pleads a grievance to linesman Ray Scapinello, while Oilers assistant captain Luke Richardson looks on. The Canadiens thought Turgeon had put the puck in the Edmonton net, but no goal was called. Referee Bill McCreary is on the phone upstairs to the video replay judge, who is reviewing the tape. The ruling is made in Montreal's favor, and they are awarded the goal. Introduced in 1991-92, video replay has since resolved many questionable goals.

Denis Brodeur

ICE LEVEL   Pre-game

Arena staff transport the goal nets out to the ice surface. All NHL nets are the same size – four feet high by six feet wide – and are carefully inspected by officials just prior to the game and at the start of each period to ensure there are no holes in the twine that might lead to controversy if a puck were to slip through.

Michel Gravel

Previous pages

GOAL JUDGES BOX   *2nd Period*

Curtis Joseph remains strong in the net, facing a flurry of
16 Montreal shots in the second period. Here, he snakes out
his catching glove to snare a shot, while Canadiens Vincent
Damphousse (left of the net) and Valeri Bure (behind the
net) lie in wait. Oilers defenseman Jiri Slegr stands at his
goalie's side to sweep away any rebound.

Andre Pichette

This page

COMEBACK   *2nd Period*

Top: *Falling behind, the Canadiens send out reinforce-
ments as (left to right) Saku Koivu, Brian Savage, and
Lyle Odelein leap over the boards.* Bottom: *Montreal fans
start to smile, as their heroes come back to tie the game
late in the second period, with hometown boy Vincent
Damphousse scoring his 33rd and 34th goals of the season.*

Andre Pichette

STRIKING OIL

2nd Period

The clear standout of the match was the play of Oilers Jason Arnott. A superstar in the making, Arnott has yet to make the breakthrough heralded by his rookie season in 1993-94, when he led the team with 33 goals and finished second to Devils goalie Martin Brodeur in Calder Trophy voting. On a night like tonight, when Arnott scored three goals in the first period (his 22nd, 23rd, and 24th of the season) and added two assists, it is clear his ascension to the top ranks of NHL forwards will not be long in coming. With the Canadiens having tied the game 4-4 before the end of the second period, and coming on strong early in the third, Arnott sets up left-winger Dean McAmmond for the go-ahead goal at 9:24. Center Todd Marchant adds another at 15:35 to give the Oilers a 6-4 lead. Chasing Arnott is Pierre Turgeon (left) who leads his team in more ways than one: as captain, and as top scorer with 36 goals coming into tonight's game.

Andre Pichette

Above

LAST MINUTE

3rd Period

Excitable Montreal head coach Mario Tremblay jumps up onto the bench to follow the play, as the puck goes into the Oilers end of the rink and regulation time draws to an end. The Canadiens do score one goal – by Patrice Brisebois at 19:55 with Habs goalie Jocelyn Thibault off for an extra attacker – but it's too little, too late, as the Oilers hold on for the 6-5 win.

Andre Pichette

F10 VR10 ANH–STL

F11 VR13 SJ–CGY

Dynasty Building

Success in professional sports is an elusive quarry. Great players may close out their career without ever being part of a championship team. Some teams just click, winning the Cup without the benefit of a bona fide superstar, through a miraculous coming together of good fortune, happenstance, and hard work. Others generate a winning mystique and an irresistible momentum of their own, meshing superior skills and a sense of destiny to perform consistently at an exalted level. Those few teams become known as dynasties, acknowledged royalty perceived to be somehow different from the rest. Joining the league in 1967-68, the St. Louis Blues had quite a start. Anchored in goal by future Hall of Famers Glenn Hall and Jacques Plante, they won two West Division titles in their first three years, and reached the Stanley Cup Finals every year from 1968 to 1970. Yet since then, in spite of a succession of talented players, the Blues have not had a glimpse of the Stanley Cup. • To a franchise hungry for a Cup, a talented team lacking that indefinable quality needed to push them to the peak, one option is to seek to acquire it by signing players who have already made it to the top of the mountain. For St. Louis Blues president and CEO Jack Quinn and general manager/head coach Mike Keenan, this course of action seemed attractive. Had the same strategy not worked in New York for Keenan two years earlier? The Rangers had stacked their roster with veterans from the Oilers dynasty of the mid- to late-eighties. Each had at least one Cup win to his credit. All knew what it took, that magical blend that results in a championship. And it had worked, bringing the Big Apple its first Stanley Cup since before Pearl Harbor. • In St. Louis in the winter of 1996, rumblings out of L.A. caused Quinn and Keenan to stir. Wayne Gretzky would be a free agent at the end of the season. The Kings seemingly were committed to a youth movement. Blues top scorer, Brett Hull, a close friend of Gretzky, began to dream of how many goals he might be able to score with the greatest passer in the history of hockey putting the puck on his stick. So negotiations began, and on February 27, Wayne Gretzky became a Blue. • In the weeks that followed, the Blues began to look like "Oilers South," as players from the Edmonton Stanley Cup years gathered in St. Louis: Glenn Anderson, a natural scorer a few goals shy of his 500th NHL marker; Geoff Courtnall,

a consistent performer on the left wing; Craig MacTavish, who was also part of the New York Rangers Cup-winning drive in 1994; goalie Grant Fuhr, at this point in the season boasting a career-best sub-3.00 goals-against average in this, his 16th NHL season. • Up to March 23, the results had been indeterminate, with Gretzky and Hull struggling to find the proper chemistry to meld their styles, and the Blues not putting together the immediate winning streak that had been anticipated. Meanwhile St. Louis fans filled the new Kiel Center to see the legendary no. 99 play for the hometown team, and root for the foundation of a new dynasty.

Facing page

US ICE SPORTS COMPLEX   *11:00 am* **CST**

Damage control: Blues general manager and head coach Mike Keenan (left) and associate coach Roger Neilson talk over last night's game – a 6-1 shellacking at the hands of The Mighty Ducks of Anaheim. The team has made a number of roster changes in recent months, and it is important that team chemistry be in place if the Blues are to advance in the playoffs. Between the two of them, Keenan and Neilson have the tools for the job: Keenan was behind the bench for the New York Rangers' 1994 Stanley Cup triumph, and Neilson, who joined the Blues this season after a two-year stint as the Florida Panthers first head coach, led the Vancouver Canucks to the Cup final in 1982.

Lynn Goldsmith

Above

BLUES EXECUTIVE OFFICES   *10:30 am* **CST**

Saturday is the only day St. Louis Blues president and CEO Jack Quinn doesn't wear a tie at the office. Quinn points with pride to a painting done by celebrated sports artist Leroy Neiman in 1968: the first of three consecutive years the Blues reached the Stanley Cup finals. The Blues have not made it as far since, but, this season, the team has made moves designed to take them to hockey's Holy Grail.

Lynn Goldsmith

BLUES PRACTICE
12:30 pm CST

Wayne Gretzky sits flanked by a couple of tough guys, Basil McRae (left) and beefy left-winger Tony Twist (right). Gretzky owns every significant scoring record in the NHL, regular season and playoffs. The Blues hope that he will lend them some of the magic that he used to lead Edmonton Oilers to four Stanley Cups in five years in the mid- and late-1980s.

Mark Buckner

ADD ICE AND STIR
1:10 pm CST

Key ingredients in the Blues recipe for success. From Wayne Gretzky (left), the team expects leadership, playmaking ability, and that indefinable quality that has made him the best hockey player of the modern era. They hope he will re-ignite the scoring talent of Brett Hull (second from left), which led him to 70-plus goal seasons from 1990 to 1992. Adding to the mix will be the steadiness and leadership qualities of center Craig MacTavish (second from right), and the offensive contributions of left-winger Geoff Courtnall.

Mark Buckner

THE PUCK STOPS HERE
1:15 pm CST

Goaltender Grant Fuhr is enjoying a career year, and that is saying a lot. As an Oiler, Fuhr was in the net for four of Edmonton's championship seasons. This year, at the ripe old age of 33, he has a goals-against average under 3.00 – better than in any of his Stanley Cup years – and the 30 wins he has recorded so far is his best tally since 1988.

Mark Buckner

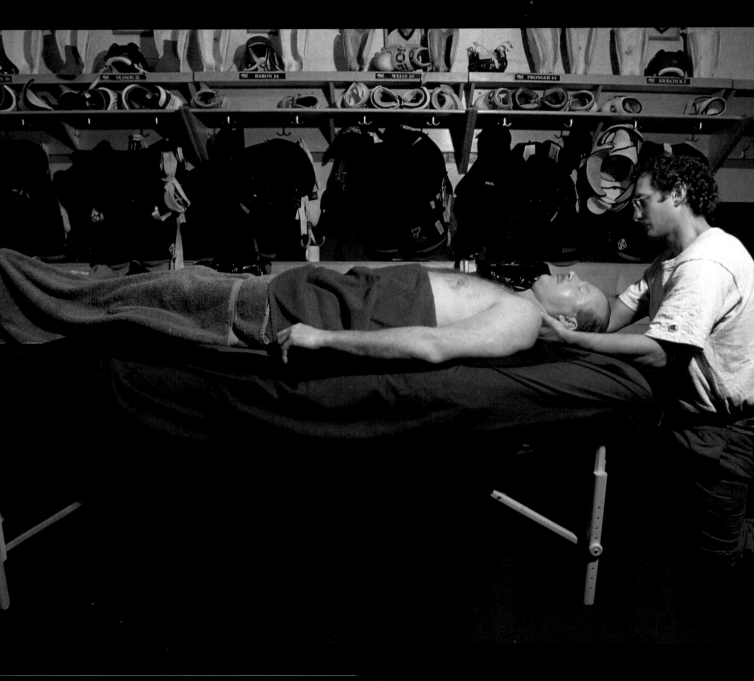

LOCKER ROOM   *2:15 pm* **CST**

...the tensions of his dual role as head coach and general manager mount
...ike Keenan can find solace at the hands of Blues massage therapist Jeff
...It's the little daily rituals that help focus the mind on the task at hand.

...oldsmith

NO. 99   3:30 pm **CST**

How many times, over his 18 professional seasons, has Wayne Gretzky signed his name, in his clear, distinctive handwriting, the number 99 notched in the loop of the "y"? Personal appearances and promotional endeavors are an important part of a superstar's life. Here, he takes a break atop a pile of signed sticks and jerseys during an autograph session at the Ritz Carlton Hotel in St. Louis.

Lynn Goldsmith

HOME COURSE   8:00 pm **CST**

Golf is more than a passing interest for Brett Hull. It has become a consuming passion, so much so that Hull has had a special "golf room" built onto his house, where he can practice his chipping and putting. On this night away from the rink, Hull and some college buddies work on their game.

Lynn Goldsmith

Blue-Collar Heroes

It was just about midnight on March 22 when the bus carrying the Buffalo Sabres rumbled out of downtown Buffalo toward the New York Thruway and Interstate 79, and – four hours off in the darkened distance – the sleeping city of Pittsburgh. Estimated time of arrival: four o'clock on the morning of game day. Call it the ultimate blue-collar road trip for a blue-collar team. ● You hear about a life of luxury in the NHL, but even million-dollar centermen and trophy-winning goaltenders aren't immune to the occasional brief bus tour of North America. Especially between New York and Philadelphia, Boston and Hartford, Long Island and Washington, Montreal and Ottawa, Buffalo and Pittsburgh. ● Yet, this little journey is peculiar – and extreme – because the Sabres have just emerged from a bruising three-hour game with the Montreal Canadiens on home ice at the Memorial Auditorium. What seems like an endless night continues with the four-hour ride to Pittsburgh, where, in a little more than 18 hours, the Sabres will have to strap on their pads again and do battle with the Penguins, who are merely the no. 1 team in the Northeast Division and Eastern Conference. ● Pittsburgh-Buffalo showdowns, in any sport – be it Penguins-Sabres, or Steelers-Bills – always seem to offer some charm. That's because the cities and the fans are cut from the same mold: old-style, blue-collar places, where you carry a lunchpail, grit your teeth, brave the elements, and put in a full day's work. The two cities are diamonds of the Rust Belt. Their fans are good, loyal, hard-working people who demand excellence; or, at the very least, a little honest sweat on every shift. On paper, the matchup doesn't promise excitement. The Penguins, led by the NHL's top three scorers in Mario Lemieux, Jaromir Jagr, and Ron Francis, have virtually clinched a playoff spot. The Sabres' talent well is not so deep. Ten games under .500, and realistically, if not mathematically, out of the playoff race, they figure to offer little resistance, especially in their second game in two nights, especially after riding the bus. ● A mismatch? On paper, yes. But looks can be deceiving in the NHL. "They've got good players and a lot of toughness," Lemieux says shortly after the the Penguins morning skate, paying proper respect to tonight's opponent. "And they've got Hasek. A great goalie. He will be a challenge." ● Once the game starts, the Sabres dip into their reservoir of adrenaline and stun a sellout crowd. Goals come from Brian Holzinger, Matthew Barnaby, Mike Wilson, Brad May, and Randy Burridge – blue-collar players all. Unflappable Sabres goaltender Dominik Hasek stops Mario Lemieux in an electrifying one-on-one penalty shot showdown. And the Sabres head for the locker room and the showers – and, eventually, the bus – with a 7-5 upset victory. ● "The penalty shot was a big lift," Burridge tells a TV interviewer, "and what a dream for the fans. The best in the league offensively against the best goalie. What a dream." A dream? A nightmare? A mismatch? An upset? A penalty shot? A bus ride? Just another day in the life of the NHL.

Facing page

SUPER MARIO   *3rd Period*

This season, Penguins superstar Mario Lemieux and his teammate Jaromir Jagr have turned the league's scoring race into a personal contest. Going into tonight's game against Buffalo, they rank one-two in points and are neck-and-neck in goals, with 57 and 56, respectively. In line to win his fifth Art Ross Trophy as the league's leading scorer, Lemieux is the only player to have won the Ross, Hart, Calder, Smythe, and Masterton trophies.

David Klutho

Top	*Bottom*
ON THE BUS *1:45 am* **EST**	**SABRES LOCKER ROOM** *6:00 pm* **EST**
Whiling away the hours, playing cards on the bus carrying them overnight through a snowstorm to Pittsburgh are Buffalo Sabres (left to right) Bob Boughner, Darryl Shannon, and Mark Astley. Shannon started the season in Winnipeg, but a mid-February trade brought him to the Sabres.	*Still emerging from the effects of a long night of travel, the Sabres gather pre-game for a meeting led by assistant coach Don Lever. If they are to have any realistic chance of making the playoffs, the Sabres will have to dig deep to dredge up their last reserves of ability, competitiveness, and professional pride for the rest of the season.*
Bill Wippert	**Bill Wippert**

As the day of the game progresses, many key individuals play an integral role in putting on an NHL game. Top left: *Assistant equipment manager A.T. Caggiano hangs game jerseys in the Penguins locker room. A.T has been with the franchise since its inaugural season in 1967.* Bottom left: *Penguins mascot "Iceberg" gets a costume adjustment. A fan favorite and cheerleader, Iceberg adds to the fun and color of a Penguins game.*

Andy Levin

Top right: *Linesman Dan McCourt stretches in the officials' room. Dan is the brother of former NHLer, and one-time Buffalo Sabre, Dale McCourt.* Bottom right: *Program vendor Bob Schiulli has been selling his wares along the concourse at Penguins games for years.*

Andy Levin

PLAYERS' BENCH   Pre-game

*Penguins Petr Nedved (left) and Jaromir Jagr, and Sabres (left to right)
Brent Hughes, Dominik Hasek, and Matthew Barnaby crack a smile as the
anthem is being sung. Brimming with unrealized potential in previous NHL
stops in Vancouver, St. Louis, and New York, Nedved has really come into
his own since coming to Pittsburgh. He enters tonight's game with 37 goals,
one short of his career high.*

NATIONAL ANTHEM   Pre-game

*Anthem singer Billy Price, lead singer of the Keystone Rhythm Band, a popular
local R&B and jazz band, offers his own stylish rendition of the national anthem.*

David Klutho

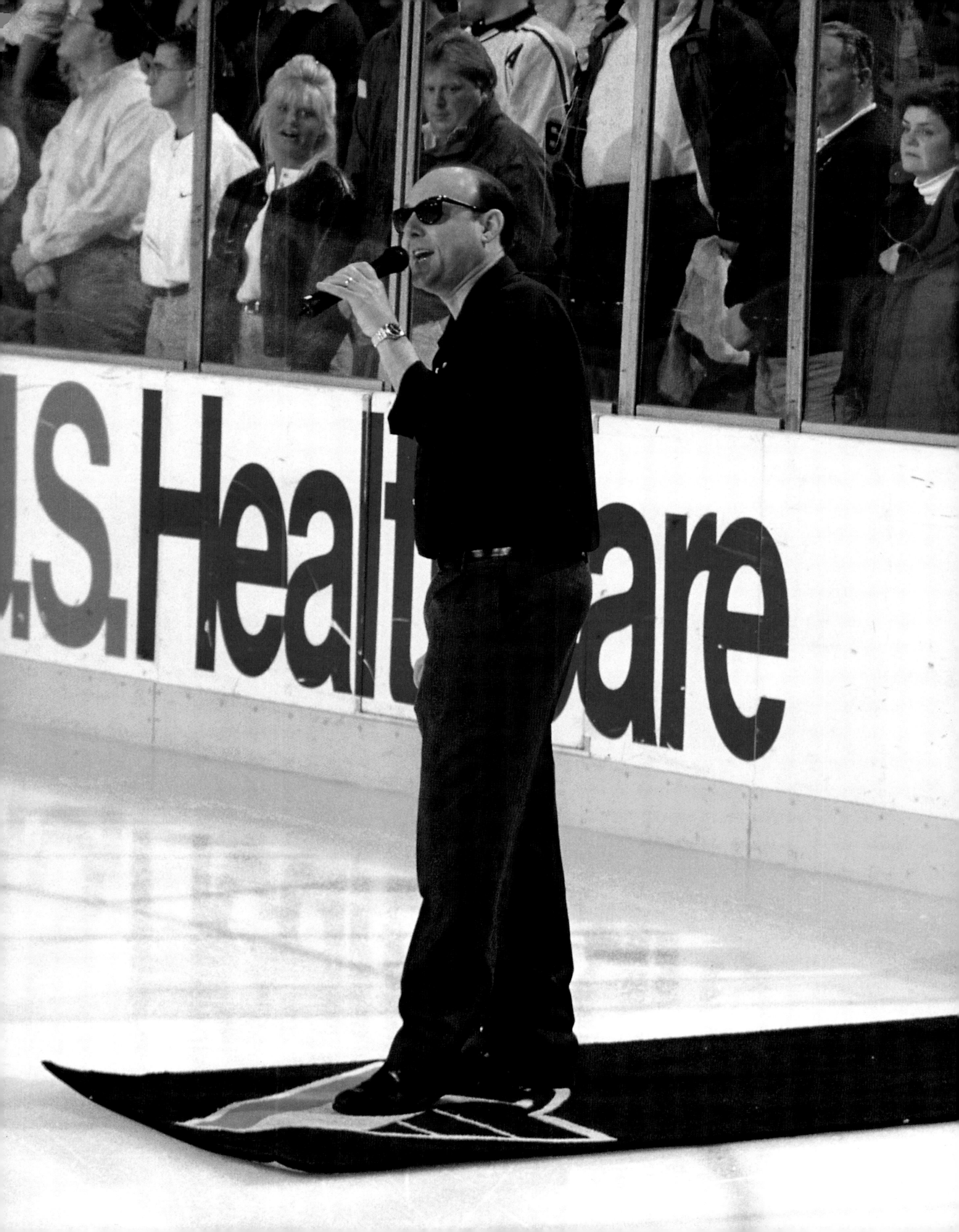

Facing page

FLAT OUT 1st Period

Flat on his face to smother the puck, Sabres goaltender Andrei Trefilov gets help from defenseman Alexei Zhitnik. Both Russians entered the NHL in 1992-93 – Trefilov with the Calgary Flames, and Zhitnik with the Los Angeles Kings – and both came to Buffalo last year.

David Klutho

This page

CHANGING OF THE GUARD 2nd Period

Trefilov struggled from the start, and after he let in two soft goals in quick succession to give Penguins a 5-4 lead, he was relieved of his misery. Top: *At 13:13 of the second period, the Sabres no. 1 goalie Dominik Hasek skates into the nets.* Bottom: *The Sabres fortunes change immediately. Jaromir Jagr, who had scored the first Pittsburgh goal just 46 seconds into the second, is stymied on his next chance by Hasek.*

David Klutho

Top, center, and bottom: *The game's
defining moment came at 5:37 of the third
period, when referee Rob Schick awarded
Pittsburgh a penalty shot against
Dominik Hasek because Hasek had thrown
his stick. Barely two minutes earlier, the
Sabres had tied the game 5-5. It was a
one-on-one showdown for the ages: the NHL's
best offensive player, Mario Lemieux, in a
quick test of skills with the league's best
goaltender, crowd standing, outcome in the
balance. Lemieux, arguably the best break-
away man in league history, has connected
on five of six career penalty shots, stopped
only by Bill Ranford, then of Edmonton,
in 1992. But he has had trouble with Hasek
in normal game situations before. After a
tantalizing pause, Lemieux approaches the
puck at center ice, swoops across the blue line,
takes a brief glance at Hasek, makes his
move, tries to slip the puck between Hasek's
legs … and is stopped. Stunned silence.
"Save!" they yell in the broadcast booth.
"Dominik Hasek! He beats Lemieux!"
The Sabres mob their delighted goalie.*

Bill Wippert

David Klutho

Previous pages

RELENTLESS PRESSURE   2nd Period

*The Sabres continue to keep the Penguins off
balance. Defenseman François Leroux falls
in front of a shot, while Barrasso flings himself across the crease, and Lemieux and Dave
McLlwain look on helplessly.*

David Klutho

Bill Wippert

The Penguins are rattled by the Sabres comeback, and circle the wagons around their unsettled goaltender, the usually steady Tom Barrasso, who backstopped them to two Stanley Cups in 1990-91 and '91-92. A Boston native, Barrasso in 1984 was the first U.S.-born player to win the Calder Trophy since the Bruins Frank Brimsek, another goalie, took home the honor in 1939.

David Klutho

After the Sabres draw even on a goal by Derek Plante at 3:11 of the third period, their captain, Pat LaFontaine, puts them into the lead at 6:05. The goal is LaFontaine's 34th of the season and 437th in his distinguished career. Hasek holds off the Penguins the rest of the way, and Randy Burridge seals the outcome with an empty net goal at 19:48. The night belongs to the blue-collar Sabres, 7-5.

David Klutho

On winter mornings, thousands of Wayne Gretzkys, Mark Messiers, and Patrick Roys are off to the rink, where thousands of other superstars-in-training await, ready to face off. For them, the dream is alive of some day making it in the NHL. Above: *In a way, it is Walter Gretzky who is responsible for NHL hockey's dynamic growth in popularity in recent years. It was Walter who taught his first son, Wayne, to skate, who flooded a backyard rink – the "Wally Coliseum" – so that Wayne could practice hour upon hour. Though his son has long ago grown up, Walter retains a strong interest in junior hockey. On this day, he is in Erie, Pennsylvania, watching a junior tournament* **CHRISTOPHER WAHL**. Facing page, left to right, from top row: *Bryan Lewis, the NHL's director of officiating, referees novice hockey in his neighborhood, Georgetown, ON* **ARNE GLASSBOURG**; *Western Hockey League Kamloops Blazers, Kamloops, BC* **PERRY ZAVITZ**; *peewee hockey player, Viking, AB* **BILL FRAKES**; *ex-NHL player and Chicago Blackhawks coach Darryl Sutter, coaching his son's team, Viking, AB* **BILL FRAKES**; *ex-NHLer and broadcaster Howie Meeker at a girls' hockey game in Parksville, BC* **ALAN ZENUK**; *U.S. Women's National Team training camp, Colorado Springs, CO* **PAUL CHESLEY**; *Outdoor Hockey League for kids playing indoors on a cold day in Regina, SK* **JUDY GRIESEDIECK**; *Morioka peewee team from Japan, at a tournament in Victoria, BC* **ALAN ZENUK**; *"Hockey Night in Boston" All-Scholastic High School Hockey Tourney, Boston, MA* **DAMIAN STROHMEYER**; *Ice Hockey in Harlem, Lasker Rink, New York, NY* **ANDY UZZLE**; *dressing for the game, Zackheim household, Westport, CT* **MICHAEL MELFORD**; *coach Joe Criscuoto with Mighty Mite team, Wonderland of Ice, Bridgeport, CT* **MICHAEL MELFORD**; *ex-NHLer Phil Goyette with the South West Island Devils Special Olympics floor hockey team, LaSalle, PQ* **TEDD CHURCH**; *mini-minor hockey game, held between the first and second periods, Vancouver-Calgary game, General Motors Place, Vancouver, BC* **KENT KALLBERG**; *members of the 1996 Esso Women's National Championship team, Moncton, NB* **PAUL DARROW**; *Joe Bucchino, general manager of IHL Atlanta Knights, with his son, David, Marietta, GA* **GREG FOSTER**; *Youth League State Championship, Littleton, CO* **DAN SINCLAIR**; *"Squirts" (9-10 year olds), Marietta, GA* **GREG FOSTER**

For many people involved with hockey, be it work or play, participating in their favorite sport translates into an all-encompassing love for the game. Hockey is a lifelong passion, and for them, it is an end in itself. Above: *When you're young, you don't need a rink to play hockey. All you need is some sticks, a few good friends, and a ball to chase. On a suburban street in Edmonton, Alberta, the neighborhood kids face off. Left to right: Keith McKay (in goal), Quinlan Winton, Matthew Lantz, Kailey Winton* **BILL FRAKES**. Facing page, left to right, from top row: *celebrated artist Ken Danby with a recent print "Bobby Orr – Garden of Dreams," Danby Mills, ON* **ARNE GLASSBOURG**; *Jason Cantwell, Cape Spear lighthouse, NF* **PAUL DARROW**; *Cody Beder, card collector, Toronto, ON* **ANDREW STAWICKI**; *Kelly Campbell, board of directors, U.S. Hockey Hall of Fame, Eveleth, MN* **LAYNE KENNEDY**; The Hockey News, *hot off the presses, Montreal, PQ* **MARIE LOUISE DERUAZ**; *NHL Central Scouting's Gary Eggleston at "Hockey Night in Boston" All-Scholastic High School Hockey Tourney, Boston, MA* **DAMIAN STROHMEYER**; *Howard Dill, Long Pond, N.S., where legend says hockey began in the early 1800s* **PAUL DARROW**; *Manon Rheaume, the only woman ever to play in an NHL exhibition game, in transit, Detroit International Airport, Detroit, MI* **WILLIAM STRODE**; *surfside roller hockey, Santa Monica, CA* **AARON CHANG**; *members of The Mighty Dirt Bags wheelchair hockey team, Los Angeles, CA* **AARON CHANG**; *wide-eyed young fans, Chicago, IL* **RICHARD BELL**; *Michael Weber, 10-year-old hockey announcer, with Glen Juniper (left) and Craig Foster (right), Owen Sound, ON* **ARNE GLASSBOURG**; *weekend warriors, (left to right) Paul Falconer, Nelson Beaton, and Chuck Reid, Britannia Community Centre, Vancouver, BC* **PERRY ZAVITZ**; *Louise St-Jacques, Stanley Cup engraver, Montreal, PQ* **MARIE LOUISE DERUAZ**; *Alphonse the Alligator, Louisiana IceGators mascot, greets Logan Willis and his mom, Karla, CAJUNDOME, Lafayette, LA* **GREG FOSTER**; *Hockey Hall of Famer Rod Gilbert and his wife, Judy, at home, New York, NY* **MARK S. WEXLER**; *Joshua Pedroza, Disney GOALS, Anaheim, CA* **AARON CHANG**; *ex-NHLer Lou Nanne (left) with son, Marty, who is a Florida Panthers scout, St. Louis Park, MN* **LAYNE KENNEDY**.

The Long Goodbye

Hockey history is winding down in Winnipeg. Eleven more times – plus playoffs, if they can get there – the players will pull on that jersey with the JETS across the chest. Then they'll store it carefully away with the memories, and put themselves on the road to Phoenix. Perhaps more than any other city, Winnipeg helped change the face of hockey. Now it is changing again. Next year, the Jets will become the Coyotes. • It's not going to be easy, saying goodbye. The faithful core of Jets fans feel a painful irony in the fact that soaring player salaries have played a part in making it impossible for Winnipeg to support an NHL franchise. For it was here that the first step was taken that made those salaries possible: the move by Winnipeg Jets Ben Hatskin, the strength behind the formation of the rival World Hockey Association in 1972, to spirit Bobby Hull away from the Chicago Blackhawks for an unheard-of $2.1 million, giving the WHA instant credibility, and triggering pro hockey's Seven Years War. When it was over, the WHA was gone and the Winnipeg Jets, Edmonton Oilers, Quebec Nordiques, and New England Whalers had been absorbed by the NHL. But the salary structure and competition that had been created was alive, well, and growing. • Those early WHA days were a heady experience for Winnipeg fans. Bobby Hull scintillated, scoring 50 goals in 50 games in 1975 to match Maurice Richard's historic pace. The Jets won three AVCO Cups – in 1976, '78, and '79 – as league champions. But a few years earlier, in 1973, a trend was established that would come to characterize the Jets franchise throughout its history. With the signing of Swedish superstars Ulf Nilsson and Anders Hedberg, Winnipeg embraced a European style of play – a heavy emphasis on speed and puck-handling ability over sheer size and strength – that remains to this day. Russian-born center Alexei Zhamnov and, until his departure in a late-season trade, Finnish winger Teemu Selanne exemplified this tradition on the 1995-96 roster. Canadian-born Dale Hawerchuk, who led the team for nine seasons through the eighties, was cut from the same cloth. For 14 seasons, from 1981 through 1995, Swede Thomas Steen defined the form. His consistency, professionalism, and dedication made him the quintessential Jet. • But these are now just fond memories. March 23 finds the team in transition: on one hand battling to reach the playoffs for their Winnipeg fans this year, on the other hand building for a future in Phoenix. In a sense the exodus has already begun. On February 7, General Manager John Paddock traded away Winnipeg crowd-favorite Selanne to Anaheim, parting with an established superstar in exchange for blue-chip 19-year-old building blocks Oleg Tverdovsky and Chad Kilger, who, he hopes, will become new favorites of a new fan base. • The Jets can accept that. Hockey is hockey. But each time they look up in the stands at Winnipeg Arena they see more white jerseys, more signs saying thank you and goodbye. Tomorrow afternoon they will play Colorado, cutting the home games left to three. It's another playoff incentive: getting there would at least delay the final farewell.

Facing page

LAST HURRAH   *12:15 pm* **CST**

Only four more regular-season home games remain in the life of the Winnipeg Jets. With the team on the move to Phoenix at season's end, fans turn out for one of their last opportunities to meet the players. Southward-bound Dave Manson, a bruising defenseman who is a tower of strength on the Jets penalty-killing squad, will be a fan favorite wherever he plays.

Wayne Glowacki

Undeterred by cold temperatures and a cutting north wind, a young fan intercepts Jets Keith Tkachuk on his way into the Winnipeg Arena for their morning skate. Destined to be the cornerstone of the new Phoenix Coyotes franchise, Tkachuk, who is closing in on 50 goals this season, has developed into one of the premier power forwards in the NHL. The logo on his cap suggests his thoughts are already drifting southward.

Wayne Glowacki

Teppo Numminen, who quarterbacks the Jets power play, tests a stick to make sure it has the right feel. Each player readies on average three to five sticks per game in case of breakage. Numminen's hard, accurate shot from the blue line has gained him four power-play goals so far this season, and he has set up many more for Tkachuk and Zhamnov. Despite the team's struggle, its power play ranks in the top 10 in the league.

Wayne Glowacki

Hard at work, players' and trainers' kids Brent Muni (left), Josh Manson (at back), and Denver Wilson (foreground) have fun and make themselves useful by running full water bottles back and forth to the bench.

Wayne Glowacki

PRACTICE   *11:15 am* **CST**

Head coach Terry Simpson has the players' full attention as he explains the focus of today's session. The Jets playoff hopes are still alive, but they must stave off the late-charging Oilers and Mighty Ducks to secure a place in post-season play. It's the coach who usually takes the blame when a team fails to live up to its potential, whether or not it's his fault. This year, as they have for 10 of the last 15 seasons, the Jets seem set to finish the season under .500.

Wayne Glowacki

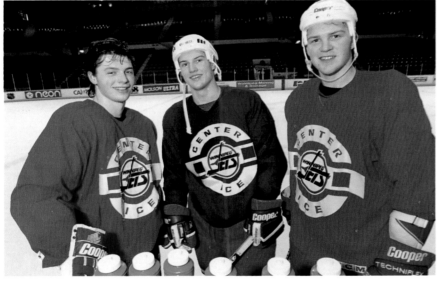

Above

A BRIGHT FUTURE   *12:00 noon* **CST**

Oleg Tverdovsky, Shane Doan, and Chad Kilger (left to right), all of them 19 years old, represent the future of the Phoenix Coyotes franchise. Tverdovsky, a factor in the Selanne trade, is a future blue-chip blueliner from Ukraine who starred with the Russian national junior team. Right-winger Doan was Winnipeg's first-round pick (seventh overall) in the 1995 Entry Draft. Kilger, also part of the Selanne trade, at six-foot-four, 210 pounds, and still growing, has great potential to be a prominent power at the center position.

Wayne Glowacki

Top

LADY IN RED

4:00 pm EST

There was a time, in the Cold War days, when Russians and North Americans were mortal enemies in the international hockey arena. Now, both prosper as teammates in the NHL. The arrival of quality hockey players from the former Soviet Union has changed the way NHL hockey is played, their speed and playmaking ability meshing perfectly with the North Americans' boldness and scoring talent. One of the first people who helped thaw relations was Anna Goruveyn, business manager for Hall of Fame goaltender Vladislav Tretiak, whose stick she holds here at her home in Toronto. She is active in representing players from the former Soviet Union and Eastern Europe, including the Jets' Oleg Tverdovsky. The jersey she is wearing was the one Tretiak wore in his last competitive game. Until he gave it to Anna, it was on display at the Red Army Museum in Moscow.

Paul Orenstein

Above

NEW BEGINNINGS

3:00 pm EST

A promising future of another kind is cradled in the arm of Alexei Zhamnov, Jets first-line center. Daughter Nicole, just two weeks old, is the focus of her father's attention today. On the injury list with nerve inflammation in his lower back, Zhamnov is able to spend time at home. He finished last season third overall in NHL scoring, behind Jaromir Jagr and Eric Lindros. This year, the Jets sorely miss him for their late-season drive to the playoffs.

Wayne Glowacki

Back at the Arena, the unsung heroes of the Jets equipment crew are hard at work.
The players get all the glory, but every franchise depends upon its support staff
to take care of the multitude of day-to-day tasks that underlie what the fans see
on the ice. Left: *Equipment manager Craig "Zinger" Heisinger tends to the*
players' uniforms. Right: *Trainer Stan Wilson sharpens skate blades according*
to each player's preferences. A keen set of blades is essential to a player's speed
and mobility on the ice. Each NHLer keeps a couple of extra pairs of skates
handy for each game in case of damage, especially on the road. Sliding into a
goalpost or the boards might nick a blade, therefore a top-notch skate-sharpener
becomes a prized asset for a team.

Wayne Glowacki

Hockey in the Sunbelt

FLORIDA PANTHERS VS TAMPA BAY LIGHTNING • THUNDERDOME, ST. PETERSBURG • GAME TIME: 7:35 PM EST

Mike Caputer had long since given up on trying to sleep. So as dawn broke on what would be a heavenly Saturday in Tampa Bay, Caputer hopped out of bed and began rummaging through a closetfull of sports equipment, pulling out a pair of in-line skates and a hockey stick. Today, he was headed for NHL BREAKOUT '96 – a traveling street and roller hockey tournament, when he might have been pulling out a pair of baseball spikes and a bat. Caputer, 12, plays center field for Mr. Willey's Royals of the Bloomington Little League, and today was game day: Field 2, 11:30 a.m. Normally, that's all Caputer would have on his mind early on a Saturday morning. But not today. Today, almost all Caputer could think of was hockey and how at 11:30 he was going to be at Busch Gardens skating in a game for the Fox Run Hawks, his neighborhood roller hockey team, against a backdrop of zebras, giraffes, and twisting roller coasters. "I hope the guys on the baseball team don't need me today," he said. "I'd like to be there, but I couldn't miss this." • The eagerness displayed by Caputer and many others like him toward NHL BREAKOUT '96 clearly displayed Florida's growing fascination with "the Coolest Game On earth." More than a thousand players representing 132 teams signed up for the tournament. Many of those teams came from far outside the Tampa Bay area to play. For the NHL, BREAKOUT is one way to introduce fans new to the sport to the basic elements and rules of hockey. • The key to long-term fan loyalty, however, is success on the ice, and although both Florida franchises are new to the NHL – the Lightning are in their fourth season, the Panthers in their third – both have established themselves as two of the league's hardest-working teams. From a standing start, they have built themselves into legitimate playoff contenders. Both teams have benefited from strong, experienced management. Panthers president Bill Torrey, who built the New York Islanders dynasty of the seventies and eighties, has assembled an inspired blend of hardworking veterans, such as Scott Mellanby and John Vanbiesbrouck, and talented rookies like Ed Jovanovski and Radek Dvorak. Phil Esposito, Torrey's wily counterpart in Tampa Bay, has done the same. In this night's 4-2 victory over his intra-state rivals, "Espo" will get goals from journeyman team leader Brian Bradley and skillful sophomore Alexander Selivanov. • As of this day, the Lightning have drawn crowds of 20,000 or more 45 times, and the Panthers have played to sellout crowds at the Miami Arena 47 times. Those crowds are the result of the two teams' work, both off and on the ice. The Lightning and Panthers have both taken their game to the community, conducting street hockey clinics at schools, and boys and girls clubs, selling young fans on a game many didn't even know existed a few years ago. The proof that their message was getting through was right there on Rink 6 at Busch Gardens, where Mike Caputer was playing hockey on a day when he could have been playing baseball.

Facing page

BREAKOUT   *4:45 pm* EST

Outside the ThunderDome, 15-year-old John Berry runs to catch one of his favorite players to request an autograph on his stick. It has been a full day of hockey action in the Sunshine State, starting with the NHL BREAKOUT '96, a street and roller hockey tournament, and concluding with a clash between Florida's two new NHL franchises.

Ben Van Hook

Top

POTVIN SPORTS 7:55 am **EST**

Hall of Famer Denis Potvin welcomes
the first customers to Potvin Sports, his
Fort Lauderdale-area sporting goods store.
Florida Panthers jerseys are popular, but
he has a soft spot for New York Islanders
jerseys bearing no. 5: the number – now
retired with honor – that he wore proudly
through 15 NHL seasons and, as the
Islanders captain, through four successful
Stanley Cup campaigns. Potvin retains
another connection to hockey. Later in the
day, he will hop an airplane to cover the
Panthers-Lightning game as the Panthers'
broadcast analyst for the Sunshine Network.

Hans Deryk

Above

POOLSIDE 1:25 pm **EST**

At his Tampa-area home, Lightning's star defenseman Roman Hamrlik, selected first overall in the 1992 NHL entry
draft, relaxes poolside before beginning his preparation for tonight's game. At this point in the season, the three-year
veteran Hamrlik, still just three weeks shy of his 22nd birthday, stands second on his team – and sixth among all
NHL defensemen – in scoring. At a rugged six-foot-two and 200 pounds, he is also the Tampa Bay Lightning's
all-time leader in career penalty minutes.

Ben Van Hook

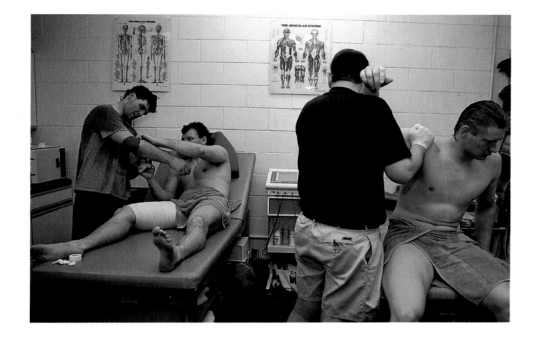

Playing with pain is commonplace, when so much is at stake at this point in the long NHL season. Getting back in the lineup is paramount on every injured player's mind, but rushing the return from an injury might risk more permanent damage. To advise them in assessing a player's progress, and to provide the hands-on therapy required, each NHL team enlists the aid of a group of medical professionals who travel with the team or treat them when they are at home – and who ensure that the players receive the best in state-of-the-art medical care. Top: *Jason Weimer works with teammate Rudy Poeschek (left), while Chris Gratton undergoes a manual therapy treatment from trainer Larry Ness to ready him for tonight's contest.* Center: *Michel Petit does a set of abdominal crunches in the weight room, with the balance ball – a staple of many sports injury clinics – working both the abdominals and back muscles without putting pressure on the back. The ball helps to improve balance and coordination so much that physiotherapists use it to rehabilitate stroke patients.*

Ben Van Hook

During the morning skate, Panthers head coach Doug MacLean (left) and general manager Bryan Murray discuss their team's performance. The pair, whose association dates back to the late-eighties when Murray was head coach, and MacLean an assistant with the Washington Capitals, have this season taken the Panthers to new heights. The third-year Florida franchise has surprised many, and on this date stands fourth overall in the Eastern Conference, poised to make an impact in their first appearance in post-season play.

Hans Deryk

Above

MOBILIZING THE TROOPS   4:45 pm **EST**

Outside their hotel, where they returned after their morning skate for a pre-game meal and rest, the Panthers board a bus that will take them to the ThunderDome to prepare for the night's game.

Hans Deryk

Previous pages

NHL BREAKOUT '96   3:00 pm **EST**

Across town at Busch Gardens, NHL BREAKOUT '96 is well underway, as players hang over the boards to follow one of the games in progress. Teams gathered from throughout the Tampa Bay region, from Clearwater to Bradenton, and as far afield as Orlando. Winners were decided in 16 age categories, from under-eights to adults, and each winning team's members received stylish NHL BREAKOUT jerseys. From Tampa, BREAKOUT '96 moves on to tour 15 other NHL cities throughout the summer months.

Ben Van Hook

Ben Van Hook

Ben Van Hook

Hans Deryk

Jonathan Hayt

Top left: *The players aren't the only ones who must loosen up for the night's action. In the officials' room prior to game time, referee Andy Van Hellemond stretches his leg muscles as part of his last-minute warm-up. Those legs have carried Van Hellemond, one of the most respected senior officials, up and down the ice in more than 1,700 regular-season and playoff games over his 25 years in the NHL.* Bottom left: *A quarter-hour before game time, Lightning assistant trainer Bill Cronin removes a box of game pucks from the freezer. He will take them to the timekeeper's box at rinkside, where they will be kept on ice until they are needed. Pucks are frozen, 30 at a time, to reduce their bounce. Overall, the NHL uses approximately 25,000 pucks in a full season.*

Top right: *Tampa Bay's ThunderDome is the only NHL arena with both an ice sheet and an amusement park under one roof. Those who will soon be cheering from the stands relax before the game in Fan Land, where hockey related tests of skill and just plain fun lend a festive air. With the bright smile of this vendor, Greg Brown, sales of cotton candy are brisk.* Bottom right: *Tonight's ceremonies begin: a color guard of children from the SunCoast Girl Scout Council precedes the arrival on ice of the game's national anthem singer.*

Top: *The smile on this boy's face means the Tampa Bay Lightning and NHL hockey have won over yet another Floridian heart.* Center: *In the pre-game warm-up, Panthers veteran goaltender John Vanbiesbrouck locks his skate over top of the boards to stretch out his leg muscles. He'll need to be agile tonight to beat his team's intrastate rivals.* Bottom: *Tampa Bay captain Paul Ysebaert hopes he will be able to lead by example again tonight: he already has scored two goals in the six games the Panthers and Lightning have played so far this year. Two nights previously, he scored a goal against Washington – his first since returning from a 24-game injury layoff.*

Glenn James

Glenn James

Facing page

THE CAT   1st Period

Poised to spring. Vanbiesbrouck sets up in the Florida Panthers goal as the teams line up at center ice, collecting his thoughts and giving his pads a last-minute check before the first puck drops. Selected first overall by the Panthers in the 1993 NHL expansion draft, he has more than lived up to his billing as a goalie to build a franchise around. Coming into tonight's game on a three-game winning streak, Vanbiesbrouck has allowed three goals or less in 32 of his 37 starts this season.

Hans Deryk

Jonathan Hayt

GAME ACTION   *1st Period*

*The Panthers struck first on a late-first-period power-play goal. The lead swung
back and forth in the second – first Tampa Bay's Petr Klima, then Florida's Ray
Sheppard, then Lightning Alexander Selivanov scored goals.* Left: *Tampa Bay
goaltender Daren Puppa plays a strong game, but lets in a first-period goal on
this shot by Martin Straka that sneaks across the line. Puppa hopes to celebrate
his 31st birthday tonight with a win, and his chances are good: going into the game,
he currently has the league's best save percentage at .921.* Top: *Panthers rookie
left-winger Radek Dvorak eludes two Lightning pursuers – Rudy Poeschek and
Patrick Poulin. Taken by the Florida Panthers 10th overall in the 1995 NHL
entry draft, Dvorak's 13 goals so far this season is ninth among NHL rookies.*
Bottom: *Lightning left-winger Patrick Poulin dodges a Panthers poke check.
Still getting accustomed to playing with his new teammates, Poulin was acquired
at the March 20 trading deadline from the Chicago Blackhawks, with defenseman
Igor Ulanov, for Enrico Ciccone. A fast learner, tonight he earns an assist on
Brian Bradley's third-period marker that will stand up as the game-winning goal.*

ONE THAT GOT AWAY

2nd Period

A scene too familiar on this night for the Florida Panthers: Vanbiesbrouck and defenseman Robert Svehla watch helplessly as the rubber hits the twine, courtesy of Lightning right-winger Alexander Selivanov, at 12:01 of the second period.

Jonathan Hayt

LIGHTNING STRIKES

3rd Period

The outcome was quite different tonight for the men in white helmets. The Lightning celebrate as Rudy Poeschek scores an empty-net goal – his first goal of this season – to break the spirit of the hard-pressing Panthers at 19:31 of the third period. The Lightning prevailed 4-2, their first win against the Panthers this season. For now, at least, Tampa Bay's playoff dreams are still alive. For the Panthers, it's time to regroup and focus on tough games in the upcoming week against the Rangers and Penguins before they get another crack at reclaiming the bragging rights from their Sunshine State rivals next Saturday night, this time in the Panthers' own home rink.

Once and Future Champs

Like most expansion teams, the Ottawa Senators must dream of Tomorrow. But the Senators have an edge. They have a Yesterday. • The first team to bear the name of Ottawa Senators was a force to be reckoned with in the early years of this century. They had won two Stanley Cup titles, in 1909 and 1911, before there even was a National Hockey League, following a tradition established by the fabled Ottawa Silver Seven, who won it four straight years starting in 1903. • The Senators were on the scene, with the Montreal Wanderers, Montreal Canadiens, and the Toronto Arenas in 1917, as one of the original four franchises when the NHL was born. For the next 10 years, they were strong contenders, winning four more Stanley Cups in 1920, '21, '23, and '27. If they paused to look back and study the history of the name their jerseys carry in this current incarnation, the young lions of today could identify with the pioneers of the game who were superstars a half-century before the term was coined. • Many are now enshrined in the Hockey Hall of Fame. Francis "King" Clancy, the artful defenseman, began his career in hockey with the Senators, then grew to greater glory with the Toronto Maple Leafs, leading that team to its first Stanley Cup in their new Maple Leaf Gardens in 1932. Frederick "Cyclone" Taylor, who contributed to the Senators 1909 Cup win, went on to lead the Vancouver Millionaires to that city's only Stanley Cup victory – so far – in 1915. Cy Denneny, the stocky left-winger, was a member of five Stanley Cup winners, first with Ottawa, then Boston. Jack Adams, a Senator for the 1927 Cup: his name is synonymous with the mid-century glory years of the Detroit Red Wings, where, as coach and manager, he led the Wings to seven Stanley Cup victories over 35 years. All are names to dream about from the days when the game was young. • These players wouldn't recognize their game today, with its high tempo, short shifts, million-dollar contracts, and worldwide stage – a game you can see without ever leaving home, through the miracle of television. And they would be amazed by the

Facing page

A VISIT TO MARSHY'S   10:30 pm **EST**

Retired-NHLer Brad Marsh raises the Stanley Cup over his head, something that he never had a chance to do during his 17-year NHL career, which ended with the Senators after their first season in 1992-93. On the move for a promotional tour from the Hockey Hall of Fame, the Cup finds itself at the end of the day at Marsh's establishment, located in the Corel Centre. The Cup came to Ottawa for the Senators' annual charity fundraising Carnival where, for a donation, fans could have their picture taken with it.

Stephen Homer

rink the Senators play on – an 18,500-seat palace called the Corel Centre. Looking down – or maybe up – what would they give to come back and skate in a marvel like that? • On this date, the present-day version of the Senators are mired in the league basement. But the young talent is coming on. Radek Bonk, Alexei Yashin, and Daniel Alfredsson all show flashes of brilliance. Despite his team's losing record, netminder Damian Rhodes has kept his goals against average among the 10 best in the league this season. Swedish rookie Alfredsson, on this date, leads all NHL rookies in scoring. • There's enough raw talent on the roster that Ottawa fans can dare to add a new word to Yesterday and Tomorrow – Soon ...

SENATORS LOCKER ROOM

9:45 am EST

Players start to arrive for practice. Goaltender Damian Rhodes (far right) has shone since being acquired January 23 as part of a three-way deal with Toronto and the New York Islanders. In Toronto, Rhodes was stuck in a backup role behind Felix Potvin. In Ottawa, he is no. 1 and since coming to Ottawa has ranked in the top 10 league-wide in goals against and save percentage, despite the Senators losing record.

Stephen Homer

Above

AHEAD OF THE CURVE

10:00 am EST

Pat Elyniuk flames his stick with a propane torch to make it malleable so he can bend it into the desired curve. Curving the blade makes it easier for the player to lift the puck, and can add an element of unpredictability to its flight, which might stymie the goaltender, much as a knuckleball can fool the batter in baseball.

Stephen Homer

COREL CENTRE   *11:15 am* **EST**

Just prior to their morning skate, players stretch out their leg muscles. Leg injuries are most common among hockey players, and the most potentially harmful to their professional careers, since a strong, swift skating ability is essential to keep up with the phenomenal pace of an NHL game. Practice can take up a fair chunk of an NHL team's "off day." Players take part in a blend of stretching, warm-ups, aerobic conditioning, skating, shooting, and puck-handling drills, as well as team meetings and focused sessions targeting aspects of team strategy such as the power play.

Stephen Homer

Above

INTENSITY   *11:30 am* **EST**

Players like Damian Rhodes work hard, even in the short skating session. The rigors of playing nearly 82 regular-season games in six and a half months – not to mention pre-season and post-season play – mean that players must maintain a high degree of physical conditioning.

Stephen Homer

129

FAMILY RESEMBLANCE

Veteran defenseman Frank Musil shares a moment rinkside with his daughter, Dina, and his son, David. Musil, who was an early season addition to the Senators from the Calgary Flames, is a reliable, stay-at-home defenseman who is seldom caught up ice. This season, he is the Senators nominee for the Bill Masterton Trophy, awarded annually by the Professional Hockey Writers' Association to the player who "best exemplifies the qualities of perseverance, sportsmanship, and dedication to hockey."

Stephen Homer

ON THE WAY BACK

While his teammates skate, center Ted Drury works out on a weight machine as part of his rehabilitation from a nagging sprain to his left wrist. Boston-born Drury, with his third NHL franchise in three seasons, was an NCAA All-American playing for Harvard University.

Stephen Homer

WHEELS

Ready to head home after a day at the rink, Radek Bonk poses with his "wheels" in front of the Corel Centre. Barely 20 years old, this native of Kmov in the Czech Republic is already in his third season in North American professional hockey – he joined the International Hockey League's Las Vegas Thunder when he was only 17. At six-foot-two, 203 pounds, and still growing, Ottawa expects Bonk to mature into an assertive, playmaking center.

Stephen Homer

*On a Saturday night at the official residence of the leader of Canada's Parliament,
the affairs of state can wait. When* La Soirée du Hockey *is broadcasting les
Canadiens against the Edmonton Oilers, Prime Minister Jean Chrétien takes a
break to follow the fortunes of a sport he has enjoyed since childhood. When he was
12 years old, he started a bantam hockey club in his hometown of Shawinigan,
Quebec. He and his teammates used Eaton's mail order catalogues as shin pads.*

Paths to Glory

So many years later, the dream remains the same: of one day playing in the NHL. All that changes are the dreamers themselves and the way their dreams are realized.

There once was a time, back in the old six-team NHL, when kids became the property of teams at an early age. You could be playing peewee hockey in Toronto, but belong to the big-league Maple Leafs. ● The Leafs' best prospects graduated to the junior Marlboros, a team they owned and operated, or St. Michael's College, a Catholic high school in Toronto regarded highly for its hockey program. ● Over the years, many a great NHL player studied at St. Mike's, including the likes of Dave Keon and Frank Mahovlich of the Maple Leafs. And some of the most entertaining hockey played was on Saturday and Sunday afternoons at the Gardens, before the Leaf games, when St. Mike's and the Marlies would play junior doubleheaders. ● It all began to change in the sixties with the arrival of expansion and the amateur draft, which spelled the end of the sponsorship of junior clubs. Then came the advent of European players. While the dream remained the same, the route to the NHL was no longer predetermined. So many years later, Eric Lindros, the budding superstar of the Flyers, the can't-miss prospect, faced a drastically different scenario after playing his junior B hockey with St. Mike's. ● "I practiced with that team when I was 14 years old," recalls Lindros. "It was a great team to play with, especially for a young guy like me. They taught me a lot on and off the ice." Some things, of course, never change. Unlike the man he now plays for, Flyers general manager Bob Clarke, Lindros entered the NHL having attained a special status. He was a superstar in waiting. Clarke, on the other hand, was just another kid from Flin Flon, Manitoba, who, because he was small and had diabetes, had no guarantees he would make it. ● Clarke did manage to walk into his first training camp as a 20-year-old and earn a job. Lindros would have done the same, but instead decided to take a circuitous route to the NHL. Drafted first overall from the Oshawa Generals by the Quebec Nordiques in 1991, Lindros refused to report to the team, and sat out from the NHL for one year. "Eric had the ability to challenge the draft," says Leafs assistant general manager Bill Watters. "From the

Facing page

"ST. MIKE'S"   *12:30 pm* EST

St. Michael's College School enjoys a storied past as the source of Hockey Hall of Fame talent. Archivist Father William O'Brien stands in front of the school's Wall of Fame, displaying photographs of some of the 141 former students who have gone on to greatness in the NHL.

Nigel Dickson

time he was 16 people knew he would be a dominant player. He was educated, he came from a strong family, and he played the bluff. He went through a tough time, but it probably matured him." ● There remain some scars from Lindros's experience, but there are no regrets. The conflicts, he says, were unfortunate, but, ultimately, he realized his dream. So his troubles are behind him, along with a splendid Saturday night at Maple Leaf Gardens. On this night, with family and friends watching, Lindros earns a couple of assists as the Flyers earn a 4-0 victory over the Leafs, a team that once upon a time would have owned his rights.

FATHERHOOD   *8:15 am* EST

Wendel Clark greets the day with two-week-old daughter Kylie Lee, Wendel and Denise's first child. The past month brought a welcome homecoming of another sort for Clark. One of the most popular Leafs ever and a former team captain, Clark had spent last season with the Quebec Nordiques and, until March 13, this season with the Islanders. Reunited with his former teammates and fans, Clark will be counted on to add spirit to a flagging club. In his first game back, on March 15 against Dallas Stars, Clark was named the game's first star, scoring the game-winning goal and adding an assist.

Andrew Stawicki

FAMILY TIME   *11:30 am* EST

Mathieu Schneider, who came to the Leafs from the Islanders along with Clark, hoists his 13-month-old son, Jared, on his shoulder. Schneider scored his first two points as a Leaf three nights earlier, picking up two assists against the Red Wings. Solid on defense and a force on special teams, his 37 power-play points going into tonight's contest leads the team.

Andrew Stawicki

Facing page

THE KIDS   *12:30 pm* EST

Kirk Muller relaxes before lunch at the hotel they have been calling home since coming to the Leafs in January with two of his three daughters, two-year-old Bryelle (left) and five-year-old Brittany, whose twin sister's name is Courtney. Any day now the Muller family will finally get settled in their new home. It's all part of being an NHL player.

Andrew Stawicki

*A joyous jumble of memorabilia surrounds Angelo Savelli in his Hamilton,
Ontario, sports collectibles store, "Canada's no. 1 King of Sports Cards." A well-
known collector of historic hockey artifacts, Savelli has complete card sets from
1909, as well as notable sticks, pucks, skates, and jerseys. March 23 happens to be
his birthday, so he is dressed for the occasion in pre-1920 hockey helmet and gloves.*

Nigel Dickson

HOCKEY HALL OF FAME

This is it – the Stanley Cup. An object of veneration for all hockey fans, the dream of every young boy who aspires to play hockey, "Lord Stanley's mug" is the basic reason why 26 NHL teams play 1,066 regular-season games each year to qualify for a chance to drink from this cup at playoffs' end. First awarded in 1893 by Canada's governor general, Lord Stanley of Preston, whose interest was piqued by his two hockey-playing sons, it is the oldest trophy competed for by professional athletes in North America. It predates even the NHL, which assumed the exclusive right to compete for it in 1926. This afternoon the Cup is on display in the Hockey Hall of Fame, in Toronto.

William DeKay

SPORTS RADIO

Sports talk radio is a trend of the nineties. One of the biggest such shows is called, appropriately enough, "The Big Show," hosted by former Leafs general manager Gord Stellick (right) on Toronto radio station The Fan 590. Today, Stellick' guests are Carl Lindros (left), Eric's father, and Gord Kirke (center), Eric Lindros's lawyer.

MAPLE LEAF GARDENS

Putting an NHL game on ice requires a high level of professionalism behind the scenes, and *Maple Leaf Gardens* benefits from one of the most experienced supporting casts in hockey. *Maintaining a flawless sheet of frozen ice in an arena, now chill and empty, that will soon be warmed with the heat of 15,746 cheering fans, is an art in itself.* Left: *The ice-making crew shovels excess ice shavings from the ice sheet, so that the rink will remain billiard-table level.* Top: *Zamboni driver Sam Deangelis has honed his craft over 28 years at the Gardens.* Bottom: *Courteous but firm in monitoring crowd behavior, Maple Leaf Gardens ushers meet with their supervisor to discuss their duties as the first fans start to arrive.*

Andrew Stawicki

Bryce Duffy

Bryce Duffy

Bryce Duffy

Andrew Stawicki

HOCKEY NIGHT IN CANADA

Pre-game

The Canadian Broadcasting Corporation's cross-Canada television broadcast,
Hockey Night in Canada, *first hit the airwaves on November 1, 1952,*
direct from Maple Leaf Gardens. Since then, every Saturday night during
the regular season and playoffs, families throughout the country have gathered
around their sets to watch their "national game." The day starts early
for Toronto's broadcast crew. Top left: *Director Jim Marshall puts the*
day's shooting schedule up on the board in the CBC's in-arena studio.
Top right: *Cameraman Jim Bawks secures the "Netcam" – a miniature*
TV camera that gives viewers a goalie's-eye-view of play – to its mount
on the net. Bottom left: *A TSN TV crew pre-tapes segments for the U.S.*
cable network, ESPN, featuring broadcasters Tom Mees (left) and Darren
Pang. ESPN will broadcast tonight's game throughout the United States.
Bottom right: *Arena announcer Paul Morris, a fixture at the Gardens*
for 35 years, has never missed calling a single Leafs home game from
his high-tech aerie high above the ice surface.

William DeKay

Andrew Stawicki

Andrew Stawicki

Andrew Stawicki

Pre-game

The pace accelerates around Maple Leaf Gardens as the players and fans count down to the first face-off. Now the oldest surviving NHL arena, the Gardens was built by Conn Smythe, the legendary Leafs owner, in 1931 in the teeth of the Great Depression, a significant testimonial to the place hockey holds in the heart of Canadians. Top left: *Flyers John LeClair (left) and Shjon Podein take a cab from the Westin Harbour Castle Hotel to the Gardens. Left-winger LeClair is enjoying a career-best year in 1995-96, second only to his linemate Eric Lindros in team scoring with a balanced 39 goals and 38 assists. Second-line left-winger Podein, an eighth-round draft pick from his home-state University of Minnesota-Duluth, has beaten the odds to win a starting position on an NHL team.* Top right: *The Maple Leafs mascot hobnobs with fans on the concourse.* Bottom left: *Fanatical fans Jay Paul (left) and Stew McConnachie show their loyalty to their teams is at least skin deep.* Bottom right: *Confident Leafs captain Doug Gilmour leaves the ice after the warm-up. Since coming to the Leafs in January 1992, Gilmour has been the team's natural leader, on ice and off. With the recent arrival of former Leafs captain Wendel Clark, and Kirk Muller, Gilmour has been able to share some of his load in providing motivation and inspiration for his teammates.*

Andrew Stawicki

Claus Andersen/BBS

Claus Andersen/BBS

Andrew Stawick

GAME ACTION

1st Period

Early on, the Flyers are aggressive, taking the play to the Leafs.
Top left: *Flyers head coach Terry Murray (left) was a finalist for the*
Jack Adams Award as the league's best coach last season for his work in
taking the Flyers to first place in the Atlantic Division. The momentum
has continued this year, as Philadelphia is neck-and-neck with New York
Rangers in the divisional race, and ranks in the top five overall.
Bottom left: *Eric Lindros outmuscles opponent Mark Kolesar for*
the puck. He and the rest of the Flyers are hungry, having lost 4-1
to the Winnipeg Jets on Friday night.

IN THE HUNT

1st Perio

The resurgent but still inconsistent Leafs are back in the pack in the Western
Conference, and they must make the most of the remaining few games or face
an early end to their season. Top right: *The Leafs were looking for some con-*
sistent scoring punch when they acquired center Dave Gagner from the Dallas
Stars in a January trade. And he has delivered, averaging almost a point a
game since his arrival. Standing in his way here is Flyer right-winger Trent
Klatt (right) who started this season as Gagner's teammate in Dallas, until
a December trade brought him to Philadelphia. Bottom right: *Maple Leafs*
head coach Nick Beverley (center) has been a stabilizing force behind
the bench since he took over March 5 from the more passionate Pat Burns,
a multiple Adams Award winner, after the Leafs failed to recover
from a rocky start to the season.

Facing page

HIGH FLYER

Pre-game

Laden with heavy expectations coming out of junior hockey, Philly captain
Eric Lindros is now recognized as a dominant force in the NHL. At
six-foot-four and well over 200 pounds, a fast skater with soft hands,
he stands head and shoulders over his opponents in more ways than one.
Coming into tonight's game against the Leafs, Lindros, centering the Flyers
top line, has 42 goals and 55 assists, already personal career highs with

A veteran journalist from a gentler era, 90-year-old Milt Dunnell enjoys this evening's broadcast in his Toronto-area home. Now retired, Dunnell covered the hockey beat for the Toronto Star *from 1949 to 1994. The beer bottle on his TV set bears the visage of curmudgeonly Maple Leafs former owner Harold Ballard, a souvenir of Ballard's 85th birthday.*

Nigel Dickson

Center: *A Don Cherry one-liner cracks up his long-suffering co-host – and more often straight man – Ron MacLean. An award-winning broadcaster for nearly two decades, MacLean says his first love is hockey, and it shows. Apart from his professional duties on* Molson Hockey Night in Canada *on CBC, in his spare time he is a Level 5 referee for the Canadian Amateur Hockey Association.* Bottom: *With his high-necked collars and outrageous bluster, flamboyant broadcaster Cherry has turned his five-minute between-periods spot into one of the most-watched segments of* Hockey Night in Canada. *A former NHL coach with the Boston Bruins and the Colorado Rockies, the blunt-spoken Cherry has turned his often-controversial comments on players into a regular morning-after coffee-time topic for thousands of fans across Canada. He is holding his own hockey card from his Boston coaching days.*

Bryce Duffy

GAME ACTION   2nd Period

Flyers defenseman Eric Desjardins lassoes Leafs Kirk Muller in front of goalie Ron Hextall. The play of Hextall, in his second tour of duty with the Flyers after two seasons with the Nordiques and Islanders, has been an important factor in the Flyers' success this season. The team is hoping this former Vezina and Conn Smythe winner will supply the strength in net to lead them through the Stanley Cup playoffs.

Claus Andersen/BBS

IN FULL SWING   2nd Period

Doug Gilmour's 13th NHL season has been a lucky one for the Leafs' talented first-line center. Exactly three months before this night, on December 23, he scored the 1,000th point of his career, and, apart from one missed game March 20 with sore ribs, he seems to be fully mended from off-season back surgery. With 26 goals going into tonight, 11 over his last 24 games, he is on pace to crack 30 for the season.

Claus Andersen/BBS

Good Neighbors

For the modern professional sports franchise, it's no longer enough to move in and set up shop. No matter what the financial backing or quality of the team, to succeed you must not merely be in a community, you must be part of it. ● The commitment goes past the autograph sessions, the media interviews, the fan club appearances, and the other obligations that go along with being a professional athlete. In today's NHL, team members are no longer athletes who happen to live in the community. They are people who live in a community who happen to be athletes. ● As a new team in new hockey territory, the San Jose Sharks lost no time in following that precept. Their Nike Street Sharks & Parks program, organized in conjunction with local schools and youth groups, provides an opportunity for local youths to play street hockey free of charge. The Sharks "Score With School" program takes players and coaches into local schools to participate in hockey-themed workshops aimed at teaching kids the fundamentals of teamwork, good sportsmanship, and goal setting. Even the Sharks' felt-finned mascot, S. J. Sharkie, gets into the act. Star of the Sharks "Be A Sport" program, Sharkie visits Bay Area elementary schools to teach kids the benefits of good sportsmanship. These are only a few of the ways the franchise has found to give something back to the people who support them. ● On this night away from NHL play, some of the Sharks are meeting some of their neighbors firsthand. In search of a vehicle to raise money for "Next Door, Solutions to Domestic Violence" a local charity, the players' and coaches' wives and girlfriends came up with the idea of dinner parties. People in the San Jose community bid for the right to host Sharks players at dinners held on this evening. ● For players like Jeff Friesen, in his second year in San Jose from the small town of Meadow Lake, Saskatchewan, Jan Caloun, from Usti-nad-labem in the Czech Republic, or giant six-foot-five-inch defenseman Jim Kyte, born in Ottawa, it's a pleasure to find friendly folks in a big metropolis, thousands of miles from home. ● It is a unique sort of commitment, because an athlete's playing career is, in a time sense, a small portion of his adult life. His long-term, after-hockey plans may well be in another part of the country. At any moment a trade could shift him and his family to a new town, new home, new school. That very knowledge might be part of the reason NHLers take root so quickly, becoming so involved in the community around them. They know that their high profile can help focus attention on worthwhile projects, that their presence at a charity dinner, saying hello and signing autographs, can help fill tables that might otherwise be empty. It's a way they can make a difference – can truly be good neighbors – no matter where they happen to be. Hockey players learn early that wherever they are is home.

Facing page

HAMMERHEAD SPIRIT   *9:00 am* **PST**

Brimming with community spirit, San Jose Sharks fans who are members of the Hammerhead Booster Club sacrifice part of their weekend for a volunteer clean up of the public park alongside the San Jose Arena. The modernistic Arena, built on a 17-acre downtown site, has, since its opening in 1993, spurred a revitalization of San Jose's urban core. The arrival of an NHL franchise in a city benefits more than just fans and players.

Frederic Larson

Equipment crews work round the clock to keep on top of all the miscellaneous but essential details needed to keep an NHL team functioning. Top: *Direct from the airport, Sharks equipment staff unload the team's baggage in the basement of the Arena. The team played last night in Calgary, the last stop on a four-game road trip, following games in Philadelphia, Boston, and Winnipeg. Saturday is a rare day off, before the Sharks start to prepare for a four-game home stand.* Center: *Once all the equipment is unloaded, equipment staff must get ready for the day's events. Pads, skates, and helmets are stashed in players' individual cubicles, and game-worn jerseys are pulled from the players' bags for laundry.* Bottom: *Preparation for the team's next practice starts now. All the different types of tape players like to use on their sticks are arrayed in neat rows. Shortly before sunrise, the job complete, the equipment staff head home at last.*

Frederic Larson

THE FOX PUCK

11:30 am **PST**

This innovative puck, commissioned by the Fox Network, is intended to help new viewers follow the fast-moving puck on the TV screen. In the mecca of high technology – Silicon Valley – the FoxTrax developer, Rick Cavallaro (left) poses with Stan Honey, executive vice president of technology for News Corp., Fox's parent company. A computer chip inside the puck sends out 30 infrared pulses per second, each 100 microseconds long. Sensors set up around the rink track the pulses and transfer data down a fiber optic cable to a control truck parked outside. Computers in the truck blend this data with signals from more sensors on the TV cameras, then generate a graphic spot of light that precisely coincides with the puck's position at any moment.

Frederic Larson

CUPID'S DARTS

3:00 pm **PST**

Shean Donovan, a fast-skating right-winger in his first full season with the Sharks, takes advantage of his day off by catching up with his girlfriend, Teresa Sherrer.

Frederic Larson

On an evening off, 23 Sharks players attended 20 dinner parties at private homes around San Jose. Hosts of one party were Bob and Marlyn Magboo and their daughters, Lauren and Michelle. First bitten by the hockey bug when they lived in St. Louis, in the years when Scotty Bowman was making the upstart Blues a winner, the Magboos jumped at the chance to buy season tickets when it was announced that an NHL franchise would be awarded to San Jose. They have invited a couple of dozen friends who share their fascination with the NHL and are eager to break bread with Sharks first-line center Jeff Friesen – 12-year-old Lauren's favorite player – and right-winger Jan Caloun. Top left: *Excitement is in the air as friends (left to right) Jennie Mortorano, Lauren Magboo, and Audrey Miyasaka await the imminent arrival of their guests.* Top right: *Michelle and Lauren Magboo welcome Jeff Friesen and Rhonda Sulpizio (right).* Bottom left and right: *Friesen signs autographs and poses for pictures with ardent fans.*

Frederic Larson

After the main course was completed, all the players and their dinner companions for the night gathered at Lou's Village, a local restaurant, to share dessert and compare experiences from earlier in the evening. Altogether, $50,000 was raised through the event to benefit "Next Door, Solutions to Domestic Violence." Top: Genial Jim Kyte, now playing with his ninth professional hockey team – Winnipeg, Pittsburgh, Calgary, Ottawa, and San Jose of the NHL, New Haven of the AHL, and Muskegon, Salt Lake, and Las Vegas of the IHL – laughs with his new neighbors. Kyte wears a hearing aid, but he has not let his deafness impair his ability to perform in the NHL. Bottom: Owen Nolan poses for one last photograph with Audrey Miyasaka and Michelle Magboo.

Frederic Larson

153

Greetings from L.A.

Two years ago to this day, March 23, 1994, in a truly glorious moment for the Los Angeles Kings franchise, Wayne Gretzky took a pass from Marty McSorley and put it past Vancouver goaltender Kirk McLean to score his 802nd goal, becoming the all-time leading goal scorer in the NHL. Gretzky was splashed with a thousand points of flashbulb lights, and basked in the adulation of Hollywood's glitterati. Exactly two years later, those memories were like old distant friends by the time the Kings played Dallas on this night, both teams already officially eliminated from the playoffs. Wayne Gretzky is gone. So is McSorley. The heart and soul of the 1993 Stanley Cup finalist team were traded away shortly before the trading deadline of March 20. But hockey in Southern California will survive their departure. ● Spawned by Gretzky's charismatic allure, the league sank its roots into other warm-weather cities – San Jose, Tampa, Miami, Anaheim, Dallas – and fans have responded. An astute Michael Eisner, chairman and CEO of the Walt Disney Company, noting that Gretzky was doing for Southern California hockey what Joe Namath did for the American Football League, created the Mighty Ducks. Eisner's interest was piqued when his sons began playing youth hockey in Southern California, another legacy of the Gretzky effect. Previously, youth hockey in the Los Angeles area languished, probably behind archery in popularity, because there were simply not enough rinks. Now, rinks are springing up all over the Southland. ● The situation in Dallas was somewhat different. Strange as it may seem in a state better known for cactus and mesquite, a hockey tradition did exist in the Lone Star State. In the sixties and seventies, the Central Hockey League's Dallas Black Hawks regularly sold out the old 7,500-seat State Fair Coliseum for home games. Since coming to Dallas in 1993, the Stars have enjoyed better than 90 percent attendance at Reunion Arena. And new Stars owner Thomas Hicks, a strong believer in the power of promotion, has pledged to put a product on the ice that will fill those few empty seats. ● The Kings may have brought NHL hockey to L.A., but now they share the lucrative Southern California marketplace with the Mighty Ducks. Winning is the thing, and Finnish sensation Teemu Selanne, joining superstar Paul Kariya mid-season, immediately helped turn a team at first considered a novelty into a legitimate playoff contender. With the Great One gone, the Kings are looking to the future. Talented youngsters like Vitali Yachmenev, the Russian right-winger who stands second overall among NHL rookies in scoring, are balanced with dependable veterans like Ray Ferraro, acquired just a week ago from the New York Rangers, and flashy forward Dimitri Kristich. A healthy Rob Blake, sidelined this season with a ligament tear, will anchor the blue line. The faces may have changed, but it's clear that hockey is alive and well in Southern California and throughout the sunny southern United States, where fans are warmly embracing a cold-weather sport.

Facing page

DREAM FACTORY
Pre-game

Kelley Hrudey has his head in the stars – Hollywood stars, that is. The Los Angeles Kings netminder's mask mirrors the celluloid dreams of his adoptive hometown. Through seven seasons – he came to L.A. from the Islanders in the same year Gretzky came from Edmonton – Hrudey was on the set as The Great One helped make NHL hockey a celebrity-studded spectacle in Southern California. Tonight, he'll watch teammate Byron Dafoe in the nets for L.A.

Wen Roberts

It's not just kids who are autograph hunters. Outside the Forum, a long-time fan asks Byron Dafoe to sign his program. Technically a rookie, though he played 10 games over three seasons with the Washington Capitals, Dafoe has made the most of a chance to play regularly with the Kings. He has challenged veteran teammate Kelly Hrudey for the starting honors, and has been in net for 13 of the Kings' 21 victories so far this season.

Mark Richards/Contact

The Kings go into tonight's game having lost five straight. This, and the need for newly arrived players to become accustomed to the Kings' system, means that practice is not taken lightly. Yanic Perreault comes off the ice following the Kings' warm-up. Going into the game with a balanced 21 goals and 22 assists, the sophomore centerman leads the team with five game-winning goals.

Mark Richards/Contact

Dallas players Mike Kennedy and Guy Carbonneau help themselves to a buffet lunch before spending the afternoon relaxing in preparation for tonight's contest. Pre-game meals are nutritionally balanced to provide the right combination of protein and carbohydrates that will provide players' bodies with fuel for the short bursts of energy and the endurance that they will require to perform optimally in the game.

Mark Richards/Contact

Top		Bottom	
FATHER AND SON	2:30 pm **PST**	**AGENT TO THE STARS**	4:30 pm **PST**

Hollywood star Kurt Russell can often be seen cheering at Kings home games, but this afternoon finds him out supporting his favorite team: the L.A. Condors, for which his nine-year-old son, Wyatt, plays goal.

Douglas Kirkland

For agent Michael Barnett, dealmaking is a way of life. As president of IMG Hockey, he helps shape the careers, on and off ice, of many of the NHL's finest players. The jerseys of clients such as Wayne Gretzky, Brett Hull, Sergei Fedorov, Jaromir Jagr, and Alexander Mogilny take pride of place on one wall of his Brentwood office.

Aaron Chang

The Kings' day contains a myriad of group and individual activities, all centered on presenting their best face for the home crowd. Left: *A thorough pre-game stretch can go a long way to cut down on pulled or torn muscles and ligaments during play. Under the watchful eye of trainer Peter Demers (in rear corner), the Kings go through a 15-minute series of exercises to work all the major muscle groups that come into play during a game.* Top: *New arrival Ray Ferraro, who until a few days earlier wore the uniform of the New York Rangers, tapes his sticks in an unfamiliar dressing room. Coming into tonight's game, he needs only one goal to tally 400 for his career. Part of the trade that sent Jari Kurri and Marty McSorley to New York, Ferraro had to switch his jersey to no. 20. The number he wore with the Rangers – 21 – belongs to Tony Granato with the Kings.* Bottom: *Becoming part of a new NHL organization involves a lot more than simply lacing up one's skates and taking the ice. Here, Ferraro poses for his formal portrait, which will be used for team media releases.*

Gary Hershorn

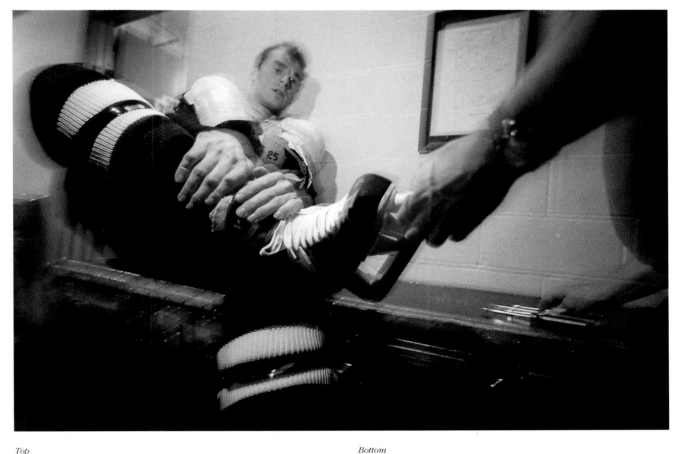

STICK WORK   *Pre-game*

Veteran defenseman Mike Lalor shapes his stick blade
with a rasp. "All the guys kid me because I do all this and
I never score," he says. It's true: his one goal scored on
March 5 ended a 110-game scoring drought. But Lalor
is not paid to score goals. His role is policing the blue line,
and in that department he has been a reliable force for
11 seasons with six NHL teams.

Mark Richards/Contact

KEEN EDGE   *Pre-game*

When Dallas Stars acquired 10-year veteran Joe
Nieuwendyk from the Calgary Flames in mid-December
and made him an assistant captain, they were looking for
leadership. That's a quality Nieuwendyk clearly possesses:
after last season he was awarded with the King Clancy
Memorial Trophy for leadership and humanitarian
activities on and off the ice. Here, his skates get a minor
tune up from equipment staff.

Mark Richards/Contact

Top: *The star of Stars, high-scoring center Mike Modano treads the tunnel from locker room to ice. With 34 goals and 70 points coming into tonight's game, Modano is having a good personal season, but his team's impending absence from post-season play puts a damper on any satisfaction he might feel. Though not mathematically eliminated, the Stars are a long shot to make it into the playoffs.* Center: *The Great One may have come and gone, but he left behind a legion of avid Kings fans – such as these wearing jerseys festooned with player signatures – who turn out to cheer on their favorite team game in and game out.* Bottom: *The long and the short of it: lined up for the national anthem, goaltender Andy Moog, five-foot-eight, flanked by defenseman Kevin Hatcher, six-foot-four (left), and Mike Modano, six-foot-three, shows that, fueled by drive and blessed by talent, a player of any size can make it in the NHL.*

Mark Richards/Contact

Mark Richards/Contact

Facing page

Play is under way, and talented Kings rookie Vitali Yachmenev looks to make a play in the Stars end of the rink during an L.A. power play. With 21 goals and 26 assists going into the game, Yachmenev stands second overall in scoring among NHL rookies.

Lee Calkins

Wen Roberts

Top

OFFICIALS' TIME OUT   *Intermission*

Between periods, hard-working on-ice officials take a breather: (left to right) linesmen Shane Heyer, referee Paul Devorski, and linesman Brad Lazarowich. Officials must be in top physical shape to skate the full 60 minutes of each game. Then, they're off to officiate another game in another city on another night.

Gary Hershorn

Bottom

POINT SHOT   *3rd Period*

His stick in position for a tip-in, Kings Ray Ferraro tries to screen Dallas goalie Andy Moog's view of a hard shot from the point. Teammate Patrice Tardif stands in position for a rebound, just outside the crease, while Dallas defenseman Mike Lalor struggles to get back into the play. In this instance, Moog was up to the task, stopping the shot.

Lee Calkins

Aaron Chang

Gary Hershorn

Danny Turner

Gary Hershorn

ON THE AIR
3rd Period

Top left: *Inside an air-conditioned trailer in the parking lot of the Great Western Forum, Bob Borgen, producer of L.A. Kings telecasts on the Prime Sports Network, calls the shots. Borgen's love for the game of hockey provides him with the inspiration required to work this pressure-packed scenario at home and on the road with the Kings year after year.* Bottom left: *Back home in Dallas, another man who calls the shots, Stars owner Thomas Hicks, enjoys the broadcast at home with three of his six children. Hicks, who assumed ownership of the team on January 19, has promised to invest whatever it will take to make the franchise a contender. Part of that investment will include a new arena, which the Stars will share with the NBA's Dallas Mavericks.*

IN PERSPECTIVE
Post-game

Top right: *Upbeat coming off the ice after his team came back from a two-goal deficit to gain a 4-4 tie, Kings head coach Larry Robinson shares a joke with Ian Laperriere, who earned the game's first star for contributing a key goal late in the first period, and assisting on Robert Lang's third-period shorthanded marker that tied the game. As a result of tonight's game, the Kings and Stars remain neck and neck in the Western Conference standings. With a winner's perspective, Robinson knows that, no matter the result, there will always be another game, and another season – another day when the Kings become a force to be reckoned with in the NHL.* Bottom right: *After the game (left to right), L.A. Kings Patrice Tardif, Philippe Boucher, and Barry Potomski cool down on the exercise bikes while watching highlights from around the league on the TV sports news. All three are in their first year with the team – Tardif arrived just weeks ago in the Gretzky trade – and all are keen to continue a winning tradition of NHL hockey in Southern California.*

Hockey, Disney Style

In the beginning there was Steamboat Willie, a cartoon starring a mouse named Mickey who was soon to conquer the world. Today there is a hockey team starring a Mighty Duck called Kariya, who looks poised to conquer the NHL. • It's easy now to say that hockey and Disney were made for one another. That, in a magic kingdom where Disney was king, the marriage of a game of fire, speed, and color, and the marketing expertise and boundless imagination of an entertainment colossus, was a match made in heaven. • Yet, remember the fuss when the franchise was born and Disney CEO Michael Eisner said he was going to call the team The Mighty Ducks, a tribute to Disney's megahit movie of the same name? • And how about the logo, the goalie mask that critics said looked like a plaster cast of Donald Duck? All it did was propel Mighty Ducks merchandise to the top seller among NHL teams. And that duck mascot, Wild Wing, descending from the ceiling, gyrating like a rock star, his hockey stick shooting flame? "This isn't hockey," the critics sputtered. "This is … SHOW BUSINESS!" • Ironically, they were exactly right. What Disney did for the NHL was what it has done for years for the film industry: Sell the sizzle. Entertain people. Make certain quality is there, that the product is a family thing and fun for all ages, but entertain! Make hockey night an extravaganza that will get the people in for a look at a game that may be unfamiliar to them. Because, once they see it, most of them will be hooked. • On the ice, go for the best. And who would fit the Disney mold better than Paul Kariya and Teemu Selanne – oozing talent, young, clean-cut, and good looking. • Away from the ice, apply the considerable resources of The Walt Disney Company to build the game at the roots level. One spin-off of Disney's new interest in hockey is making a difference in the lives of hundreds of young Californians. Disney GOALS (Growth Opportunities through Athletics, Learning and Service) gives less-privileged kids a chance to learn about the game first-hand, playing hockey together on concrete, ice, or grass, depending upon the season. The basis of the program, as organizer David Wilk explains it, was quite simple: "Kids are a fabulous resource. Let's do something with them." Disney GOALS staff also teach academic subjects, using hockey topics as the basis for assignments. And, they allow participants to learn first-hand the value of community service, giving them opportunities to help others less fortunate than themselves – helping wheelchair athletes to play hockey, or reading to sight-impaired seniors. • Show biz? Absolutely. But there's substance beneath the sizzle. Hockey may never be the same, but Disney and the Mighty Ducks are doing their best to give it a valued place in the culture and the community of Southern California.

Facing page

DISNEY GOALS   7:05 am **PST**

In the game of hockey, as in the game of life, a good grounding in athletics and learning, as well as a sense of your community, leads to success. Here, Marco Cervantes suits up for one of the early morning roller hockey games that are the basis of this popular program, sponsored by the Mighty Ducks. Founder David Wilk also established Ice Hockey in Harlem – a similar program in New York City.

Aaron Chang

THE DRAKE HOTEL, CHICAGO　　3:55 am **CST**

In the wee hours of Saturday morning, tired Mighty Ducks stroll through the lobby of their residence in Chicago – appropriately enough, The Drake Hotel. They are arriving from St. Louis, where last night they enjoyed a satisfying 6-1 victory over Wayne Gretzky and the rest of the Blues. Today is an off-day for them; tomorrow they will face the Blackhawks in a midday match-up.

Ronald C. Modra

CHILD'S PLAY　　11:30 am **CST**

Later on that day players have some free time to themselves. Better known for his physical presence on the ice, Mighty Duck Todd Ewen also has an artistic side. For Ewen, cartooning is a way of relaxing, but more than that – he has created and illus-trated a children's book starring his favorite character: a frog called Hop.

Ronald C. Modra

FULLY FLEDGED STAR　　3:15 pm **CST**

On route back to the hotel after the Ducks' afternoon practice, Paul Kariya takes in the Chicago scenery from his window seat. Picked fourth overall by the Mighty Ducks with their first-ever NHL Entry Draft selection, Kariya played for Team Canada in the 1994 Olympics, where his country won the silver medal, and in the 1994 World Championships, where it took gold. He led the team in scoring at both tourna-ments, a trend he continued in his first pro season, 1994-95, when he outscored his next closest teammate by 10 points. This season, he has maintained his scoring touch, with 42 goals and 38 assists to date, above a 1.25 points-per-game average.

Richard Bell

He may look fierce, but he's a hit with the kids. The Mighty Ducks popular mascot, "Wild Wing," poses with fans in Disney's Magic Kingdom – just down the freeway from the Arrowhead Pond of Anaheim where the Mighty Ducks come home to roost. Best known for his acrobatic on-ice routines at Ducks games, Wild Wing is also kept busy making personal appearances on behalf of the team.

Aaron Chang

PHYSIO 4:30 pm CST

The 82-game NHL season exposes players to a constant barrage of physical contact. Even players not badly enough hurt to be placed on injured reserve require constant attention to their minor aches and pains. Back at the hotel, Teemu Selanne, lying on a portable treatment table, gets a much-needed leg massage from Paddy Jarit, Mighty Ducks head athletic trainer and physical therapist, while David Karpa waits his turn, a bag of ice cooling his aching thigh muscle.

Richard Bell

DINNERTIME 7:00 pm CST

Hungry for their evening meal, (left to right) Todd Ewen, Jean-François Jomphe, Paul Kariya, and Teemu Selanne ask The Drake concierge for his recommendation on restaurants. Selanne's acquisition February 7 added luster to the Anaheim line-up. In his stellar first NHL season, 1992-93, the "Finnish Flash" finished fifth overall in scoring with 132 points, and was a shoo-in for the Calder Trophy. So far this year, his 99 points rank him among the league's top 10 scorers.

Richard Bell

STEPPING OUT 7:10 pm CST

Out on the street, Ken Baumgartner, just acquired from the Toronto Maple Leafs at the March 20 trading deadline, gets his bearings, while he and the Ducks pause to sign a few autographs. Making certain that things remain under control is doorman Carlos Ramos (right), a fixture at The Drake for many years, who is well known to visiting NHLers.

Richard Bell

Top		Bottom	

OUT ON THE TOWN — 7:15 pm **CST**

Their destination a short stroll away, the players all head off for dinner. Paddy Jarit, Teemu Selanne, and Frederic Olausson take in the bright lights of downtown Chicago.

Richard Bell

BUON APPETITO — 8:00 pm **CST**

One of the pleasures of travel for NHL players is a chance to sample the fare of the best restaurants nation-wide. Here, they consult the menu at Carmine's, on Rush Street. Left to right: Todd Ewen, Ken Baumgartner, Darren Van Impe, Selanne, and Randy Ladouceur.

Richard Bell

Making it Big

At the Calgary Flames' morning skate, Theoren Fleury looks as he always looks when the battle lines have yet to be drawn – a small and gap-toothed boy darting joyously in and out of the adults in a pick-up game of shinny, hoping none of the big people will tell him to go home. At five-foot-six and 160 pounds he is clearly too small to keep a place on an NHL franchise, let alone become its very heart. Okay, he is tiny. So is the wasp that gets trapped in your car. You're so busy flailing away at it, you don't notice the telephone pole until you hit it. Fleury is the wasp. On this night, the Vancouver Canucks will be the car. ● You could make a case that Theoren Fleury was born to be a Flame, to play in a small-market city that conventional wisdom writes off as too small to compete with the giants to the south. Hadn't he heard those same charges all his life? Too small to make it big as a junior. Too small to survive in the NHL. Can't play with the big boys. They'll eat you alive. But then, fans in both Vancouver and Calgary will tell you that when it comes to their path through the NHL, unconventional wisdom has prevailed. ● Between them the Flames and the Canucks helped write a new page in NHL history, before the 1989-90 season, by scooping the famous KLM Line as part of the first wave of talent from the Soviet Union. The Canucks got Igor Larionov and Vladimir Krutov, the Flames took Sergei Makarov, and the face of North American hockey was forever changed. Four times in the past 15 years teams from these two cities have made it big, reaching the Stanley Cup Finals – twice each – with Calgary the champions in 1989. Through the first half of the nineties, no other team in the NHL has played more playoff games than the Vancouver Canucks. But the struggle to survive and compete, in a country where team income is in Canadian dollars and many players' salaries in American, is never-ending. ● To survive, Canucks team owners opted to shoot for the moon, reconfigure their ownership, build a new arena, acquire an expansion NBA franchise, and run their own show. Orca Bay Sports & Entertainment has been a dazzling success, with the Canucks and the NBA Grizzlies playing to sellout crowds. ● Back home, the Flames survived the latest crisis by gaining control of and refurbishing the Canadian Airlines Saddledome into a fine facility in its own right. But their population base is still small, the quest for season-ticket holders an

Facing page

CAPTAINS COURAGEOUS   *1st Period*

Canucks captain Trevor Linden (left) and Flames captain Theoren Fleury face off. Both players are true leaders – their grit and determination, game in and game out, inspire their teammates. The Canucks' winning percentage soars on nights when Linden scores one or more goals, and Fleury is the heart and soul of the Flames.

Chris Relke

ongoing struggle. ● Except in the sense that success means fan interest, which translates into revenue, which translates in turn, if not to optimism, at least to hope, such weighty matters are no part of existence for Fleury and the Flames once the anthem is played tonight. There's a playoff race on and a game to be played against one of the teams that could put them on the outside looking in come mid-April. ● The wasp goes into full buzz. This is one they need. Nothing less than a win will be tolerated. Fleury simply will not allow it. His shorthanded goal at 9:22 of the first period is the 2-0 backbreaker in a game that ends 4-0. For now at least, western bragging rights belong to the small-town gang from the foothills.

RAVE ON   *12:01 am* **PST**

*Still revved up after attending an exciting 5-2 Vancouver victory over the Dallas
Stars on Friday evening, Canucks superfan Andrew Castell stands amidst his
impressive collection of hockey memorabilia. At 14,000 items and counting, it
includes such treasures as a stick used by Russian goaltender Vladislav Tretiak
in the 1972 Canada-Soviet Summit Series, autographed by both Tretiak and
Paul Henderson, who scored the dramatic winning goal to beat the Russians.*

Alex Waterhouse-Hayward

SON OF A LEGEND   10:45 am PST

Fred Taylor, Jr., 80-year-old son of hockey legend Fred "Cyclone" Taylor demonstrates the merchandise at Cyclone Taylor Sporting Goods. Fred Jr. started the store, named after his famous father, in 1957. Fred Sr. led the Vancouver Millionaires to Stanley Cup victory in 1915. Annually, the Canucks present the Cyclone Taylor Award to the team's most valuable player, as voted by the fans, which was won last season by Trevor Linden.

Jason Stroud

COMFORTS OF HOME   1:00 pm PST

Back home for a rest after morning practice, Trevor Linden catches a basketball game on TV. With 30 goals going into tonight's game, Linden stands second in team scoring behind Alexander Mogilny, and seems destined to better his career high of 75 points in a season. In a game four days earlier against Colorado, Linden had scored his 500th career point, putting him third overall in Canucks career scoring, just behind Thomas Gradin and Canucks assistant coach Stan Smyl, who holds the record at 673 points.

Perry Zavitz

GAME BOYS   2:30 pm PST

Computer games are a sure way of getting the attention of today's kids, and, through the innovation of Electronic Arts (Canada), Inc., the National Hockey League is on the leading edge. Ken Sayler (right) and Adam MacKay-Smith stand in front of a screen showing one of their creations: NHL96.

Alex Waterhouse-Hayward

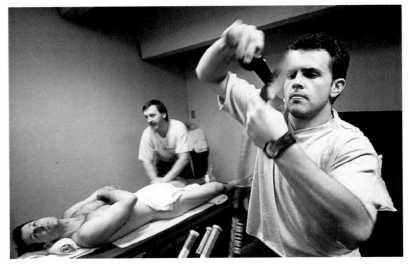

Top left: *The Flames backroom boys seem confident going into tonight's game. Left to right: Assistant coach Bill Hughes, head coach Pierre Page, and head trainer Jim "Bearcat" Murray. Page, in his first season as Calgary's head coach, previously held the reins in Minnesota and Quebec, where both NHL teams experienced dramatic upswings in their fortunes under his tutelage. He has known Murray, one of the most recognizable trainers in the NHL, since the 1980-81 season, when Page was an assistant coach in Calgary, and Murray was in his first season as trainer. Bottom left: Equipment manager Bobby Stewart improvises some repairs to a player's uniform. An equipment manager on the road needs to be a jack-of-all-trades and a master of improvisation, creating solutions to any equipment repair or replacement situations that emerge, as they so often do, when the team is away from its home arena.*

George Olson

Top right: *James Patrick gets a last minute massage from Tony Oumerof while rookie center Cory Stillman puts some finishing touches on his stick blade. Patrick came to Calgary in 1994 after 11 years on the New York Ranger blue line, and part of a season in Hartford. Since his arrival, he has made a strong offensive contribution on the power play, and has been a patient mentor for the Flames younger defensemen. Stillman, Calgary's first-round pick in the 1992 Entry Draft, has sparkled in his first NHL season, placing among the top 10 in rookie scoring. Bottom right: Stress starts to show on the players' faces in the Flames locker room as game time approaches. Left to right: Zarley Zalapski, Tommy Albelin, James Patrick, and Trent Yawney.*

George Olson

HOME ROOM   Pre-game

In a relaxed and casual manner, born of a lifetime of repetition, Canucks players
ready themselves for tonight's contest. Left to right: Hardworking left-winger
Martin Gelinas, in the midst of a career-best year, has prospered after being given
an opportunity to play regularly with the Canucks top line. Speedy right-winger
Russ Courtnall, in his first full season as a Canuck, is enjoying the chance to
play close to his hometown of Duncan, B.C. The Canucks are hopeful that
Markus Naslund, acquired just three days ago from the Pittsburgh Penguins,
will add scoring depth on either wing. Alexander Mogilny, a certified superstar,
came to Vancouver in the off-season from the Buffalo Sabres.

Robert Semeniuk

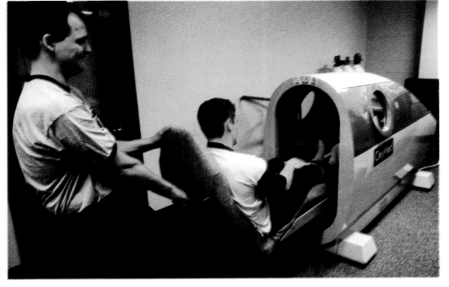

Above

HYPERBARIC CHAMBER   Pre-game

Canucks injured center Mike Ridley has a session inside the team's hyperbaric chamber.
The Canucks were innovators among NHL teams in the use of this equipment – a
sealed chamber through which oxygen-enriched air is circulated. Use of the chamber
has been found to accelerate the body's natural healing process.

Robert Semeniuk

Throughout the arena nearly 200 employees work diligently to get ready for the evening's entertainment. Top: *At the Winning Spirit sports paraphernalia shop on Level 100, staff members prepare the stock for the arrival of souvenir hunters.* Center: *At the concessions, food is being prepared to satisfy hungry fans. Food workers will pop 500 pounds of popcorn kernels to feed tonight's anticipated crowd of more than 18,000. Also on the menu, will be 1,500 hot dogs, 700 hamburgers, and 1,600 slices of pizza, all washed down by 1,400 gallons of beer, and topped off with 800 ice cream cones.* Bottom: *Mark McIntosh takes his Olympia ice-making machine for a spin around the rink to iron out the wrinkles so the ice will be at its best come game time.*

Rocky Widner

Rocky Widner

Facing page

IN THE TUNNEL   *Pre-game*

"Captain Kirk" McLean, here seen heading up the tunnel from the dressing room to the ice for the pre-game warm-up, has been steadfast as Canucks first-string goaltender for more than eight seasons. Tonight he'll watch from the bench as rookie Corey Hirsch makes the start. Since mid-January, Hirsch has been outstanding in a backup role while McLean was out of commission after having had surgery to his left knee.

Robert Semeniuk

Alex Waterhouse-Hayward

Top

RUSSIAN MAGIC   *1st Period*

Two products of the former Soviet hockey system that has contributed so many
stellar players to the NHL: Canucks right-winger Alexander Mogilny is
pursued by Flames center German Titov. Mogilny won a gold medal with
the Soviet team at the 1988 Olympics, while Titov was a member of their
gold-medal team at the 1993 World Championships. Mogilny is soaring
in his first year as a Canuck: with 53 goals, he has accounted for one out
of every five Canuck goals, but on this night he is held scoreless.

Chris Relke

Previous pages

CLOSE ENCOUNTERS   *1st Period*

Players scramble in front of the Canucks goal during a Flames power play
while defenseman Adrian Aucoin is off for interference late in the first period.
Moments after this picture was taken, defenseman Steve Chiasson scored the
Flames fourth goal of the first period.

Rocky Widner

Above

CALIFORNIA DREAMIN'   *7:45 pm* PST

While his teammates toil on the General Motors Place ice, injured Canucks winger
Pavel Bure and his friend, Dahn Bryan, relax amidst the surf and palm trees of
Southern California. Bure, out for the season with an injury to the anterior cruciate
ligament of his right knee, is in California for a short break from his rigorous
rehabilitation program.

Douglas Kirkland

On the set, Hockey Night in Canada *host Steve Armitage prepares to interview Markus Naslund on the subject of his recent arrival from Pittsburgh.*

Robert Semeniuk

Kent Kallberg

THE RIVALS   *3rd Period*

There is no love lost between the Calgary and Vancouver franchises, and tempers flare in the final period. Center: *At 3:52, linesman Wayne Bonney comes between Canucks Joe Kocur and Flames Jocelyn Lemieux. Kocur, acquired at the trading deadline from the New York Rangers, has wasted no time in making his presence felt. For his efforts he earns a two-minute highsticking penalty and a 10-minute misconduct.* Bottom: *It's a physical contest, and Flames goalie Trevor Kidd, in his third year on the team, raises an objection about the Canucks jamming his crease to referee Terry Gregson.*

Following page

FLAWLESS   *3rd Period*

During a stoppage in play, Trevor Kidd skates across to the bench. Kidd has struggled at times this season, and has shared the Flames netminding duties with Rick Tabaracci. Tonight he is hot, and the Canucks are unable to put a puck by him.

Chris Relke

Chris Relke

Rocky Widner

A STEP AHEAD   *3rd Period*

*Since being acquired from New Jersey on November 23, Canucks Esa Tikkanen –
who played on the New York Rangers Stanley Cup-winning team in 1994 – has
performed his checking role with dogged diligence, but tonight he has a hard time
keeping up with Fleury. His teammates, likewise, seem to be one step behind the
hardworking Flames all night long.*

Rocky Widner

Robert Semeniuk

DOWNHEARTED   *3rd Period*

*Inconsistency has plagued the Canucks throughout the 1995-96 season. Tonight's
scoreless effort, on the heels of a 5-2 domination of the Dallas Stars Friday night,
is all-too-characteristic.* Above left: *Dejection shows on the face of Corey Hirsch,
whose competitive spirit is irked by the loss. Hirsch played his way onto the team
when McLean was injured mid-season, and showed that he had the ability to
be an NHL starter.* Above right: *In the executive suite, Canucks president and
general manager Pat Quinn is not pleased as he watches his team run hot and
cold in the important drive for position in post-season play. Quinn contemplates
changes that may have to be made.*

*As the day draws to a close, a solitary figure performs an ongoing ritual integral to
the future of the NHL. To provide them with the field intelligence they will need to make
informed picks at the upcoming Entry Draft, NHL general managers rely upon an
army of professional and semi-professional scouts, who, each winter, attend thousands
of hockey games in hundreds of small towns across North America and Europe.
Here, Don Paarup, a scout for the Colorado Avalanche, takes careful notes during
a game between the Western Hockey League Seattle Thunderbirds and the hometown
Kamloops Blazers, Memorial Cup champions in 1992, '94, and '95. He is looking
for players possessing that special quality that will allow them to make the leap to
stardom in the NHL.*

Perry Zavitz

186

It's a wrap! Across the land, the focus shifts away from the arena, the hubbub dies down, and the lights go out on one day in the life of the NHL. Players celebrate or commiserate, trainers attend to weary muscles, coaches and management assess their team's performance. The last reporter's story is filed, as are official game reports and statistics compiled by the League. Fans who have watched the games, on TV or in person, passionately rehash outstanding plays, whether spectacular or controversial. Tomorrow will bring a new day and a different story for every NHL team. Players at rest today will have a key match-up on Sunday, March 24, while others will be on the move to play in another city, or at home preparing for their next opponent. Today's winners may be tomorrow's losers, and vice versa. The life of the NHL is filled with change and infinite variety that make each day a new challenge. The only constant is the game, where steel meets ice, stick meets puck, and players contend for victory, and for the ultimate prize – the Stanley Cup. Above: Throughout North America, late-night TV sports reports broadcast highlights from the day in hockey. Here, just before airtime, make-up artist Julie Wiktowy helps the hosts of Canada's all-sports network TSN, Gino Reda (left) and Darrin Dutchyshen, prepare for their wrap-up of NHL action on "Sports Desk" at the network's broadcast center in Toronto.

Paul Orenstein

187

Epilogue

And then, on a warm June night in Miami – 1,066 league and 86 playoff games after the start of the season – it was over. The last cheer had echoed out of the Miami Arena, the last plastic rat had been hurled, and a classy bunch of Florida Panther fans had swallowed their disappointment and risen to their feet in their own rink to give a standing ovation to a Colorado Avalanche that had buried their beloved Panthers in four straight games. ● The cheers were as much for their own team as for Colorado – and why not? The Panthers were the Little Engine That *Almost* Could, a team that had turned swarming, full-pressure defense and an unquenchable work ethic into a force that had elbowed its way into the Stanley Cup Finals. ● Now they had fallen – to a Colorado team they could match in work ethic but, in the end, not in firepower. The South Florida fans had seen a classic goaltending duel between Colorado's mid-season addition, Patrick Roy, and their own beloved "Beezer," John Vanbiesbrouck. They had seen a near-record goal-scoring performance by Conn Smythe Trophy winner Joe Sakic overwhelm the best efforts of their own hard-working Dave Lowry, Ray Sheppard, and Stu Barnes. The series may have been a sweep, but it took the Avs two full overtime periods and 4:31 of a third before Uwe Krupp finally ended Game Four with the only goal of the night. Who could have thought, back on that Saturday in March, that the Panthers or Avalanche would ever reach the Finals? Sure, the Avalanche were second in the Western Conference, but they were 22 points behind the Detroit Red Wings, destiny's apparent choice to represent the West. When the regular schedule ended, that gap had widened to 27. Over in the Eastern Conference, the Panthers were in a dogfight with the Philadelphia Flyers, Pittsburgh Penguins, and New York Rangers. "Flash in the pan," the experts predicted. "They've got no big man, no go-to guy." The Flyers had Eric Lindros and the "Legion of Doom." Pittsburgh had Mario Lemieux and "Mario Jr.," Jaromir Jagr. The Rangers had Mark Messier and so many more. Out of that trio would come a team that would give the Red Wings a run for their money. ● That was about the only question being asked as the playoffs began: Which would

Conn Smythe Trophy winner Joe Sakic   Steve Babineau

win out: the size and power of the Eastern rep or the speed and finesse of the Red Wings? The Avs and the Panthers? Get serious! So they did. The Avalanche beat Vancouver in the first round while the Panthers took out Boston. "Just wait," said the experts. The Avalanche eliminated Chicago in six. The Panthers upset Philadelphia in six. "Okay, they're on a roll," the experts said. "But now they're up against Detroit and Pittsburgh. It's over." And it was – for the Red Wings in six and the Penguins in seven. ● Suddenly, the superstars were gone and the unsung heroes were at center stage, some to prove that they should have been rated stars all along. Next season, they will be. And the chase will begin again. In the NHL, it's not the story that ends, only the latest chapter.

1:30 am EST

Posing for posterity, members of the victorious Colorado Avalanche organization, from
stars to stick boys, gather for a group portrait with the Stanley Cup. They swept the

The Photographers

Graig Abel:
Toronto

Claus Andersen/BBS:
Toronto

Brian Babineau:
Boston

Steve Babineau:
Boston

Richard Bell:
New Jersey & Chicago

Bruce Bennett:
Washington, D.C.

Paul Bereswill:
Long Island

Chris Black:
Toronto

Grant Black:
Detroit & Winnipeg

Denis Brodeur:
Montreal

Mark Buckner:
St. Louis

Lee Calkins:
Los Angeles

Jean-Marc Carisse:
Office of the Prime Minister
Ottawa

Greg Cava:
Fresno, Las Vegas & Phoenix

Aaron Chang:
Anaheim & Los Angeles

Paul Chesley:
Denver & Colorado Springs

Tedd Church:
Montreal

Paul Darrow:
Cape Spear, Moncton, St. John's, Summerside & Windsor

William DeKay:
Philadelphia & Toronto

Marie Louise Deruaz:
Montreal

Hans Deryk:
Fort Lauderdale & Tampa Bay

Nigel Dickson:
Toronto

Bryce Duffy:
Toronto

Greg Foster:
Atlanta & Lafayette

Bill Frakes:
Edmonton & Viking

Arne Glassbourg:
Georgetown, Guelph & Owen Sound

Wayne Glowacki:
Winnipeg

Lynn Goldsmith:
St. Louis

Michel Gravel:
Montreal

Judy Griesedieck:
Regina & Saskatoon

Annie Griffiths Belt:
Washington, D.C.

Dan Hamilton:
Toronto

Jonathan Hayt:
Tampa Bay

Gary Hershorn:
Los Angeles

Stephen Homer:
Ottawa

Glenn James:
Tampa Bay

Rob Johnston:
Toronto

Kent Kallberg:
Vancouver

Layne Kennedy:
Eveleth & Minneapolis

Douglas Kirkland:
Los Angeles

David Klutho:
Pittsburgh

Todd Korol:
Calgary

Frederic Larson:
San Jose

Paul LaVenture:
Westborough

Andy Levin:
Pittsburgh

Scott Levy/BBS:
Long Island

Douglas J. MacLellan:
Toronto

Constantine Manos:
Boston

Peter Martin:
Montreal

Stephanie Maze:
Washington, D.C.

Michael Melford:
Bridgeport, Bristol, Syracuse & Westport

Ronald C. Modra:
Chicago

George Olson:
Vancouver

Paul Orenstein:
Toronto

Mark Peterson/SABA:
New York City

Andre Pichette:
Montreal

Kenneth Redding:
Vail

Chris Relke:
Vancouver

Mark Richards/Contact:
Los Angeles

Michael Ridewood:
Lethbridge

Wen Roberts:
Los Angeles

Robert Semeniuk:
Point Roberts & Vancouver

Barton Silverman:
Long Island

Brian Smale:
Long Island, New Jersey & New York City

Andrew Stawicki:
Toronto

William Strode:
Detroit

Damian Strohmeyer:
Boston

Jason Stroud:
Vancouver

Danny Turner:
Dallas

Andy Uzzle:
New York City

Ben Van Hook:
Tampa Bay

Jerry Wachter:
Washington, D.C.

Christopher Wahl:
Buffalo & Erie

Alex Waterhouse-Hayward:
Vancouver

Mark S. Wexler:
New York City

Rocky Widner:
Vancouver

Brian Winkler/BBS:
Long Island

Bill Wippert:
Buffalo & Pittsburgh

Perry Zavitz:
Burnaby, Kamloops & Vancouver

Alan Zenuk:
Duncan, Esquimalt, Parksville & Victoria

We would like to thank all the photographers involved in this project – for making our lives easier by master-fully capturing the essence of their assignments, and for making our lives difficult by supplying us with more wonderful images than we could ever fit into one book.

Hockey writer: "Red" Fisher, Montreal
Michel Gravel

Stars fans: Kimberly Van Heel and Lynne Pryor, Dallas
Danny Turner

Trouble brewing: Sabres vs Penguins, Pittsburgh
David Klutho

Future stars: Peewee hockey, Viking, Alberta
Bill Frakes

A SPECIAL THANK YOU TO **KODAK CANADA** FOR THEIR GENEROUS ASSISTANCE ON THIS PROJECT. ALL PHOTOGRAPHS WERE SHOT EXCLUSIVELY ON **KODAK** PROFESSIONAL FILMS.

Kodak
PROFESSIONAL
PRODUCTS

Created and Produced by Opus Productions Inc.

President/Creative Director: Derik Murray
Vice President, Production: David Counsell
Design Director: Don Bull
Creative Consultant/Photo Editor: Brian Daisley
Photography Coordinator: Colette Aubin
Photography Assignment Coordinator: Krista Thompson
Photography Consultant/Photo Editor: Steve Fine
Visual Coordinator: Joanne Powers
Electronic Art: Joseph Llamzon, Guylaine Rondeau
Chief Financial Officer: Jamie Engen
Publishing/Logistics Coordinator: Ruth Chang
Marketing Manager: David Attard
Sales Representative: Chris Richardson
Office Manager: Catherine Palmer

Vice President/Publishing Director: Marthe Love
Senior Editor: Brian Scrivener
Executive Publishing Coordinator: Wendy Darling
Publishing Associate: Jennifer Love
Editorial Coordinator: Michelle Hunter
Publishing Assistants: Iris Ho, Allie Wilmink
Publicity/Research Coordinator: Gillian Hurtig
Research Coordinator: Beth Freeman
Research Consultant: Andrew Castell
Research Assistant: Andrew Bergant
Travel Coordinator: Abbey McGrath
Production Assistants: Elfriede Todorovich, Raj Samtani

Special Editorial Consultant: Jim Taylor

Opus Productions would like to thank the following:

NHL Enterprises, L.P.: Rick Dudley, Richard Zahnd, Ed Horne, Charles Schmitt, Elle Farrell, Mary S. Trapani, Douglas Perlman, Ruth Gruhin

National Hockey League: Commissioner Gary Bettman, Steve Solomon, Jeffrey Pash, Brian Burke, Arthur Pincus, Bernadette Mansur, Mary Pat Clarke, Gary Meagher, Benny Ercolani, Greg Inglis, Adam Schwartz, Bryan Lewis, Kelley Rosset, Frank Bonello, Gary Eggleston, Mario Carangi

CollinsPublishersSanFrancisco: Carole Bidnick, Maura Carey Damacion, Ken Fund, Paul Kelly, Jain Lemos, Terri Leonard, Carole Vandermeyde, Adrian Zackheim

HarperCollinsPublishersLtd: Tom Best, Carol Bonnett, Iris Tupholme

Hockey Hall of Fame: Jeff Denomme, Phil Pritchard, Christine Simpson

Opus Productions would like to thank all of the countless people at the 26 NHL teams who dedicated their time and energy to this project. We would also like to thank all the people at the venues who were instrumental in providing access.

The Mighty Ducks of Anaheim: Bill Robertson, Rob Scichili • *Boston Bruins:* Heidi Holland • *Buffalo Sabres:* Seymour Knox IV, Jeff Holbrook, Ken Martin Jr., Gil Chorbajian • *Calgary Flames:* Rick Skaggs • *Chicago Blackhawks:* Jim DeMaria • *Colorado Avalanche:* Jean Martineau • *Dallas Stars:* Thomas Hicks, Larry Kelly, Kurt Daniels, Lee Smith, Jouni Lehtola • *Detroit Red Wings:* Bill Jamieson, Tony Lasher • *Edmonton Oilers:* Bill Tuele • *Florida Panthers:* Greg Bouris • *Hartford Whalers:* Chris Brown • *Los Angeles Kings:* Mike Altieri, Sergio Del Prado • *Montreal Canadiens:* Ronald Corey, Donald Beauchamp • *New Jersey Devils:* Michael Gilbert • *New York Islanders:* Ginger Killian Serby, Brian Reynolds • *New York Rangers:* Neil and Katia Smith, Brooks Thomas, John Rosasco, Ann Marie Gilmartin • *Ottawa Senators:* Laurent Benoit, Brad Marsh • *Philadelphia Flyers:* Mark Piazza • *Pittsburgh Penguins:* Harry Sanders • *San Jose Sharks:* Ken Arnold • *St. Louis Blues:* Jack Quinn, Mike Keenan, Adam Fell, Rick Braunstein, Janiece Chambers • *Tampa Bay Lightning:* Gerry Helper, Barry Hanrahan • *Toronto Maple Leafs:* Bob Stellick, Pat Park • *Vancouver Canucks:* Steve Tambellini, Veronica Varhaug, Devin Smith • *Washington Capitals:* Nancy Yasharoff • *Winnipeg Jets:* Richard Nairn, Jeffrey Hecht

Opus Productions would like to thank all of the NHL players, both past and present, their families, and their agents, who gave of their time and were integral in making this book possible:

Michael Barnett, Jamie Fitzpatrick, Eddie Mio, Jiri Crha, *International Management Group* • Vladimir Bure • Don Meehan, Anna Goruveyn, *Newport Sports Management* • Howard J. Gourwitz, *Ardmore International Management Corporation* • Carl Lindros • Mary Kay Messier, *Messier Management International* • Marc Perman, *International Creative Management* • Jean Roy

Opus Productions would like to recognize and thank the writers who contributed to this book:

FRANK BROWN, *New York Daily News*, The Long Hard Road • ROY CUMMINGS, *Tampa Tribune*, Hockey in the Sunbelt • LISA DILLMAN, *Los Angeles Times*, Greetings from L.A. • PAT HICKEY, *Montreal Gazette*, The Ghosts of the Forum • LEN HOCHBERG, *Washington Post*, The New Breed • TOM McMILLAN, *Penguins Report*, Blue-Collar Heroes • NANCY MARRAPESE, *Boston Globe*, Showdown in Beantown • SCOTT MORRISON, *Toronto Sun*, Paths to Glory • BRIAN SCRIVENER, captions and additional text • JIM TAYLOR, *Sports Only* Making it Big; Hockey, Disney Style; Mister Consistency; Good Neighbors; Return to the Windy City; The Long Goodbye; Reaching Altitude; Dynasty Building; Once and Future Champs

Opus Productions would like to acknowledge the following for their contribution and support:

Sam Aceti, Andy Gorchov, Pittsburgh Civic Arena • Rejean Amyot • Carl Anderson, Marty Evtuskev, Hartford Whalers Booster Club • Joe Angeles • Ron Austen • Dave Baird, San Francisco Spiders • Bill Bell, WFTY • Rick Benej • Steve Bernstein • Tom Bitove and staff, *Wayne Gretzky's* • Matt Blaty • Bob Borgen • Claude Brière, Manon Langlois, Molstar • John Brown, John Brown Sports • John Bucyk, Boston Bruins Alumni • Joe Cadillac • Art Caldwell • Alan Campbell • Steve Carter, Bruce Connal, Anne Marie Trotta, ESPN • Peter Scarth, Brad Thompson, Tracy Chin-Sam, Rick Peterson, Kodak Canada Inc. • Joe Chiodo • Jeffrey Chong • Roger and Billy Christian, Christian Bros. • Katrina Chrzanowski • Alan Clark, John Shannon, CBC Sports • David Cohen, California Hockey Productions • Gary Cooper, Hammerhead Booster Club • Geoff Currier, CKRM • Danielle Chinnery • Rich Clarkson • John Davidson, MSG Network • Fred Dawes • Michael Day, Paul McLean, Dave Rashford, TSN • Vince Wladika, Lou D'Ermilio, FOX • Peter Donolo, Bruce Hartley, Office of the Prime Minister • Greg Douglas, *Sports Only* • Matt Douglas • Dick Drew • Bob Ducatte, Rensselaer Polytechnic Institute • Sharyn Duffy • Brenda Eng, Canuck Place • Paul Falconer • Mark Ferguson • Matthew Fineman • Tracy Girouard, Louisiana IceGators • Larry Goldstein • Linda Goodman, Don Ogden, Gayle Robson, Supreme Graphics • Heather Gore, Creative Artists Agency • Walter and Phyllis Gretzky • Bill Hayes • Charlie Hodge • Eleanor Keaton • Thom Klos • Michael Korinchinsky • Arnie Krause, Metropole Litho • Deanna Kuder • Michelle Kuitunen, U.S. Hockey Hall of Fame • Mike Lange, George Priyr, Prime Sports • Lieutenant Denise Laviolette • Baz Lee • Denis Hainault, Phil Legault, Glynis Peters, Canadian Hockey Association • Guy Lafleur • Carole Lee • Jeff Leigh • Todd Levy, Ice Hockey in Harlem • Steven and Patty Ann McDonald • Margaret McInnes • Winfield McKay • Pat McLaughlin • Jim McNelis • Glenn McPherson • Rusty Mathews, Ontario Hockey League • Stephen Minuk • Sandy H. Miller • John Muscato, Buffalo Children's Hospital • Eric Nesterenko • John Nicolls • Ross Normand • Rosaire Paiement • Chris Pasternak, New Jersey Devils Booster Club • Dino Pedecilli, Frank Selke, Canadian Special Olympics Inc. • Rod and Jim Pederson • Jerry Pfremmer • Mark Piazza • Cliff Pickles, North South Travel • John Pothitos, J.P. Goalie Masks • Gaby Renault, Steve Dryden, *The Hockey News* • Constable Rice, RCMP • Steve Rivera, Slapshots • Pat Sarma • Jim Sarosy, Syracuse Crunch • Doug Secord, Ministry of Fisheries and Oceans • Michael Simmons • Gary Smith, *Sports Illustrated* • Louise St. Jacques • Darryl Seibel, Kris Pleimann, USA Hockey • Howard Silverman • Celia Southward • Cathy Sproule, G.W.E. Group Inc. • Thomas Steen • Gord Stellick, The Fan 590 • Darren Stomp, Brians Custom Pro Mfg. Ltd. • Raphael Sugarman • Darryl Sutter • Ivano Toscani, Anchor Bar • Jason Ulmer • Roman Uschak, Michigan State University • Chad Varhaug, CKNW • John Vassallo, NESN • Brian Watson, The Penalty Box • Paula Wellings • David Wilk, Disney GOALS • Matt Wrbican, The Andy Warhol Museum

We would like to express special gratitude and sympathy to the family of the late Seymour Knox, III, former chairman of the Buffalo Sabres and a member of the Builders' Section of the Hockey Hall of Fame. Standing proudly with his son, Seymour Knox, IV, he kindly posed for this photograph in front of the new Marine Midland Arena less than two months before his passing.

Christopher Wahl

Facing page: Hockey Hall of Famer Guy Lafleur joins other all-time NHL greats as part of the Oldtimers Hockey Challenge, taking on a Calgary Police team at the Canadian Airlines Saddledome.